# The Sacrament of Easter

This book is respectfully dedicated to the Right Reverend and Right Honourable Graham Douglas Leonard, Lord Bishop of London, and the Right Reverend Eric Waldram Kemp, Lord Bishop of Chichester: true Fathers in God.

# The Sacrament of Easter

*Roger Greenacre*
*and*
*Jeremy Haselock*

*Gracewing.*

**EERDMANS**

This edition published in 1995

Gracewing                                      Wm B. Eerdmans Publishing Co
Fowler Wright Books                            255 Jefferson Ave SE
Southern Ave, Leominster                       Grand Rapids, Michigan
Herefordshire HR6 0QF                          49503 USA

First published by Gracewing in 1989, revised in 1991

*This book is distributed*

*In New Zealand by*            *In Australia by*
Catholic Supplies Ltd          Charles Paine Pty Ltd
80 Adelaide Road               8 Ferris Street
Wellington                     North Parramatta
New Zealand                    NSW 2151 Australia

Typesetting by Burgess & Son (Abingdon) Ltd.,
Thames View, Abingdon, Oxfordshire
Additional typesetting by Reesprint, Radley, Oxfordshire

Printed and bound by Redwood Books, Trowbridge, Wiltshire

UK ISBN 0 85244 134 7
US ISBN 0 8028 4099 X

# Abbreviations

ARCIC   Anglican-Roman Catholic International Commission.
ASB     *The Alternative Service Book 1980.*
EH      *The English Hymnal.*
ICEL    International Commission on English in the Liturgy.
LHWE    *Lent. Holy Week. Easter.*
NEB     *The New English Bible.*
NEH     *The New English Hymnal.*
PL      *Patrologia Latina.*
RCIA    *The Rite of Christian Initiation of Adults.*
SCR     The Sacred Congregation of Rites (now called the Congregation for Divine Worship).

The authors and publishers would like to acknowledge all the publishers and authors who gave them permission to quote from their works. Full details of the titles, authors and publishers are given in the notes accompanying each entry.

All efforts have been made by the publishers to contact copyright holders to elicit their permission before quoting from their works.

Except where otherwise stated, all scriptural quotations are taken from *The New Jerusalem Bible* (Darton, Longman and Todd, London, 1985); quotations from the Psalms, however, are taken from *The Liturgical Psalter* of *The Alternative Service Book 1980* and follow the Hebrew numeration.

# Contents

*Foreword* ... ... ... ... ... ... ... ... ... iv
*Introduction* ... ... ... ... ... ... ... ... ... vi
Chapter 1. The Lenten Journey ... ... ... ... 1
Chapter 2. The Passover of the Jews ... ... ... 18
Chapter 3. The Passover of Christ ... ... ... 35
Chapter 4. The Passover of Christians ... ... ... 52
Chapter 5. The Mystery of the Cross ... ... ... 67
Chapter 6. The Great and Holy Week ... ... ... 80
Chapter 7. The Great Fifty Days ... ... ... ... 148
Chapter 8. The Rediscovery of Easter ... ... ... 159
Index ... ... ... ... ... ... ... ... ... 171

# Foreword

From the earliest times, the Paschal Mystery has been the essence of the Church's worship and doctrine:

> The tradition I handed on to you in the first place, a tradition which I had myself received, was that Christ died for our sins, in accordance with the scriptures, and that he was buried; and that on the third day, he was raised to life, in accordance with the scriptures. (1 Corinthians 15:3-4)

The tradition of which S. Paul writes is not an intellectual agreement but a relationship that is to be lived liturgically. Through analysis and commentary, the two authors of this book show the unbreakable link between prayer and belief which is encapsulated in the maxim *lex orandi, lex credendi*. If we take this link seriously, it offers important insights as to the place of the liturgy in our present work of restoring unity between Churches and especially between the Anglican and Roman Catholic Churches. As the members of the Anglican-Roman Catholic Joint Preparatory Commission affirmed:

> Since our liturgies are closely related by reason of their common source, the ferment of liturgical renewal and reform now engaging both our Communions provides an unprecedented opportunity for collaboration. (paragraph 13 of the Malta Report, printed in *The Final Report* of ARCIC p.112).

The authors of this book are both Anglicans, but they have been careful to examine our common tradition by looking at Roman Catholic as well as Anglican liturgical texts and at the commentaries of Roman Catholic as well as Anglican (and other) authors. In addition, they requested the help of a Roman Catholic consultant who was asked to examine the text from a specifically Roman Catholic point of view. This book is at once ecumenical and liturgical in its scope and says important things about what lies at the heart of our common tradition. We commend it to members of both our Churches. We hope in particular that it will be of assistance to the clergy in their teaching and in their own personal formation towards a deepening of the Paschal Mystery in their lives.

The special quality of the power of the liturgy is well summarized in the Introduction to the Church of England's book of services and prayers *Lent, Holy Week, Easter*:

> The Holy Spirit takes the things of Christ and shows them to us. Worship has a dimension of directness but also a dimension of history and tradition. Our worship is one with the worship of the whole Church of the ages. To be a Christian is to enter into the tradition consciously and gladly. (p.2.)

We hope that *The Sacrament of Easter* will enable Christians to penetrate more fully the heart of their Christian existence and we pray that, as our two Churches together grow in real knowledge of the Paschal Mystery, the Easter victory of Christ will triumph over our present divisions.

✠ COLIN WINTON

The Rt Revd Colin James, Bishop of Winchester
and Chairman of the Church of England Liturgical
Commission.

✠ THOMAS McMAHON

The Rt Revd Thomas McMahon, Bishop of Brentwood
and Chairman of Liturgy, Roman Catholic Bishops'
Conference of England and Wales.

December 1988

# Introduction

*The Sacrament of Easter* was first published in 1965 by the Faith Press as No. IV in the series *Studies in Christian Worship*. It grew out of a sequence of Lent addresses and its publication was due in the first place to the insistence of Dr Eric Mascall, who had heard the addresses, and in the second place to the encouragement of Dr Ronald Jasper, then publishing director of the Faith Press.

That first edition was warmly welcomed, but has long been out of print. A new edition has been requested by many and it soon became clear that any such edition would need to be a very substantial revision, if only because of liturgical changes in both the Roman Catholic and Anglican Churches since 1965. Although I began this work some years ago, it only really got off the ground when the Reverend Jeremy Haselock offered his assistance. He is, however, in the fullest sense a co-author, and we take joint responsibility for the whole book.

We acknowledge gratefully the invaluable help given by our Roman catholic consultant, the Reverend David Manson of the Diocese of Brentwood; it is our hope that his help and guidance will enable our book to be of interest and usefulness to English-speaking Roman Catholics.

We are also grateful to Fr John Lee of the Russian Orthodox Cathedral of the Assumption and All Saints in London, to the Reverend Norman Wallwork, Superintendent Minister of the Keswick and Cockermouth Circuit of the Methodist Church, and to Mr Chaim Raphael, the distinguished Jewish author, and the Sisters of Sion in

Bayswater for help over the Eastern Orthodox, Methodist and Jewish traditions. Others who have helped us at particular points include the Reverend Dr Brian Horne, the Reverend Canon Roy Porter, Dr Gillian Evans, Dr Mary Hobbs, Mrs Mary Holtby and Mr Stephen Need. A special word of gratitude is due to my former secretary, Mrs Margaret Cameron, for long hours spent typing and re-typing my manuscript in its early stages, before the advent of Fr Haselock's word processor. We are grateful to our colleagues, the Dean and Chapter of Chichester and the Reverend David Perkin of S.James's, Sussex Gardens, in Paddington, for their patience and forbearance during the writing of this book. Finally, we must thank the Bishop of Winchester and the Bishop of Brentwood for their most encouraging Foreword and the Reverend Canon Geoffrey Rowell and Fr Manson for their help in making this possible.

On the back cover of the 1965 edition, the publishers printed this brief description, which we believe to be applicable also to this revision:

> This book is neither a theological study of our Redemption nor a devotional commentary on the Cross and Resurrection, but rather an introduction to the liturgical celebration of Holy Week and Easter. It is written in the double conviction that the depth of meaning of the Paschal Mystery is seriously weakened if it is not given its full liturgical and sacramental expression, and that the Holy Week liturgy demands from all who participate in it a more profound awareness of its biblical background and of its central place in the Church's life.

Chichester,
The Commemoration of S.Ambrose of Milan,
1988.
Roger Greenacre

An artist's impression of the *Anastasis* fresco in the church of
S.Saviour-in-Chora (Karije Museum), Istanbul.

*Chapter I*

# The Lenten Journey

"When a man leaves on a journey," Archpriest Alexander Schmemann of the Russian Orthodox Church has written, "he must know where he is going. Thus with Lent. Above all, Lent is a spiritual journey and its destination is Easter, The Feast of Feasts."[1] The trouble is that many English-speaking Christians have embarked many times upon Lent either without realising that it is a journey, a pilgrimage, or without being clear as to its destination.

> Forty days and forty nights
> Thou wast fasting in the wild;
> Forty days and forty nights
> Tempted and yet undefiled.[2]

This nineteenth-century composition is probably the most popular and widely used of Lent hymns, certainly among Anglicans, who are very much influenced (consciously or unconsciously) by the hymns which they sing. Lines from this hymn were recently even embroidered in large letters on a set of Lenten eucharistic vestments and altar furnishings for use in an English cathedral. Its frequent use probably reinforced the idea, which was once widespread and is still not quite dead, that Lent is to be observed primarily as a deliberate imitation of our Lord's forty days in the wilderness before the beginning of his public ministry, and that this is why it came into being.

At one time the first known reliable mention of Lent was thought to date from 325 and was to be found in the fifth canon of the First Council of Nicaea. The Greek word used in this document is *tesserakoste* which clearly indicates forty days, but it is now thought that this refers to a post-paschal period, leading up to the day later to be kept as the Ascension, rather than to a time of fasting before Easter.[3] For Lent the crucial documents seem to be the festal letters of S.Athanasius issued on the Epiphany each year to inform the faithful of the date of Easter and the beginning of the Paschal Fast. The second of these letters, issued in 330, announces the date of the beginning of a forty-day fast before Easter, incorporating within it an older six-day fast comprising the period we would call Holy Week.[4] From Athanasius's later letters it would seem that the forty-day fast was something of an innovation, resisted in some communities, but rapidly becoming universal. He makes frequent references to scriptural precedents for forty-day fasts but interestingly never refers to the fast of Jesus in this context but presents Lent purely as an extended period of ascetical preparation for Easter.[5]

Even when adopted universally, the length of the fast varied and varies still for two reasons. The first was uncertainty as to whether forty days of actual fasting were to be counted (and the Eastern Rite forbids fasting on Saturdays as well as Sundays), or merely a season totalling forty days; the second was a difference in reckoning when exactly Lent ended. So the Roman, and hence the Anglican, tradition begins Lent on Ash Wednesday; the Ambrosian Rite of Milan, faithful to a more ancient tradition, on the following Sunday (the sixth before Easter); and the Byzantine Rite (according to which Lent ends on the Friday evening before Palm Sunday and is therefore quite distinct from Holy Week) at Vespers on the seventh Sunday before Easter.

To find the real significance of Lent we need to examine its liturgy, and in this study we shall concentrate on the Roman and Anglican liturgies. Happily, the Church of England in its *Alternative Service Book* has authorized the use of the eucharistic lectionary of the reformed Roman Rite on weekdays; other Churches of the Anglican Communion have also adopted that lectionary for Sunday use but, sadly, in England the General Synod has not seen fit to follow suit[6]. A study of the Lenten liturgy reveals the dominance of three distinct but related themes. These are *Penitence and Self-Denial*; *Christian Baptism*; and *The Lord's Passion*. The readings of the ferial (weekday) Lenten masses illustrate these three themes. From Ash Wednesday until the end of the second week of Lent the first theme clearly predominates; it is illustrated by Old Testament readings such as the repentance of Nineveh at the preaching of Jonah (Jonah 3:1-10) on Wednesday of the first week, and Daniel's confession of the sins of Israel (Daniel 9:4-10) on Monday of the second week, and by Gospel readings such as the parable of the sheep and the goats (Matt 25:31-46) on Monday of the first week; Christ's call for us to be reconciled to our brother (Matt 5:20-26) on Saturday of the first week, and the parable of the prodigal son (Luke 15) on Saturday of the second week. From the third Sunday the theme of Baptism emerges more strongly; it is illustrated by Old Testament readings such as the healing of Naaman in the waters of Jordan (2 Kings 5:1-15) on Monday of the third week, and the stream of water issuing from the Temple (Ezekiel 47) on Tuesday of the fourth week, and by Gospel readings such as the three classic Johannine passages used from the earliest times for the instruction of candidates for baptism: the Samaritan woman (John 4) in the third week, the healing of the man born blind (John 9) in the fourth week, and the raising of Lazarus (John 11) in the fifth week. From the fifth Sunday the theme of the Lord's Passion predominates; it is illustrated by Old Testament readings such as the fiery serpent (Numbers 21) on Tuesday of the fifth week and by Gospel readings from the 8th, 10th and 11th chapters of S.John.

The common link between these three themes is the Feast of Easter, the liturgical celebration of the paschal mystery.[7] It cannot be stressed too emphatically that Lent does not exist for its own sake: it is nothing if it is not a preparation for Easter, a kind of corporate retreat for the whole Church militant to prepare it for participation in the paschal solemnities.

The liturgical year of the Christian Church up to the time of the Council of Nicaea and the "christianization" of the

Roman Empire by the Emperor Constantine was extremely simple. Practically its only features were a weekly and an annual *Pasch* or Passover. The content of both was the whole mystery of our redemption - and, in particular, the Passion, Resurrection and Ascension of Christ, the Descent of the Holy Spirit, and the Second Coming of our Lord. Every first day of the week, every Sunday, was from New Testament times the weekly celebration of the Christian mystery, when the People of God assembled together to proclaim in the eucharist the Lord's death on the day of his Resurrection. Sunday was not only a commemoration of the past and its actualization in the present, but also an anticipation of the End, for it was the 'eighth day', the ushering in of the new and definitive creation.

Recent reforms in both the Roman and Anglican rites have restored the primacy of Sunday as a Feast of our Lord, and hardly any Saints' Days may now be observed on Sunday. This restoration of Sunday was a principle clearly and concisely stated by the Second Vatican Council in *Sacrosanctum Concilium*, the Constitution on the Sacred Liturgy of 1963:

By a tradition handed down from the apostles, which took its origin from the very day of Christ's resurrection, the Church celebrates the paschal mystery every seventh day, which day is appropriately called the Lord's Day or Sunday. For on this day Christ's faithful are bound to come together into one place. They should listen to the word of God and take part in the Eucharist, thus calling to mind the passion, resurrection and the glory of the Lord Jesus, and giving thanks to God who "has begotten them again, through the resurrection of Christ from the dead, unto a living hope" (1 Peter 1:3). The Lord's Day is the original feast day, and it should be proposed to the faithful and taught to them so that it may become in fact a day of joy and of freedom from work. Other celebrations, unless they be truly of the greatest importance, shall not have precedence over Sunday, which is the foundation and kernel of the whole liturgical year.[8]

So much for Sunday, which a great liturgical historian of the Church of Scotland, Dr A.A.McArthur, has called "the basis of the Christian Year"[9]. Alongside this weekly celebration of the whole mystery of redemption there was an annual celebration, the Christian Passover, the *Pascha* or *Festum Festorum*. It consisted essentially of a long all-night vigil beginning after sunset and culminating with the eucharist at or before dawn. We do not know exactly how far back this goes, though some scholars have claimed to find evidence of the observance in some of the New Testament writings[10]; the clear reference to Christ as "our Passover" in 1 Corinthians (5:7) cannot be taken to imply a Christian adaptation of the Passover festival by S.Paul himself, but it would obviously have served as a potent encouragement to those who did take that step. It is possible that many early Gentile Christian communities did not observe the *Pascha* at all - especially those who contested the authority of the Old Testament and were strongly anti-Judaistic, and those who were held back by S.Paul's own criticism of the observance of "special days, and months, and seasons and years" (Gal 4:10). But if, as Thomas Talley has written, "the promulgation of annual festivals had little place in the agenda of the Gentile mission ... there would have been less diffidence (towards continuity with Passover) in the primitive community of Jerusalem, and there, we can believe, the observance of Passover continued, its ancient theme of redemption transformed by the triumph of the Paschal Lamb of the Covenant renewed."[11]

It is known that there was controversy over the date of the Christian *Pascha* during the second century A.D. The Churches of Asia Minor - the Quartodecimans - kept the *Pascha* on a fixed day of the Jewish lunar month (14th Nisan), the day on which the Jews immolated the paschal lamb; the other Churches had come to observe it always on a Sunday[12]. In about the year 155 S.Polycarp, Bishop of Smyrna, tried in vain during a visit to Rome to persuade Pope Anicetus to conform to the Asian usage; despite their continued disagreement there was no breach of communion. Thirty or forty years later Pope Victor attempted to stamp out Quartodeciman practice. When the recalcitrant Polycrates, Bishop of Ephesus, refused to conform, arguing that the Asian Churches were doing no more than faithfully continuing the tradition that they had received from the Apostle John himself, he excommunicated him, thus provoking a strong protest from S.Irenaeus, a native of Asia Minor who had become Bishop of Lyon and who pleaded for tolerance and respect for diversity.

In the years after the Council of Nicaea we find that the *Pascha*, the all-night vigil between Saturday and Sunday, had its prolongation (the great fifty days of the Pascha-Pentecost celebration) and its preparation, at first the one or two days immediately preceding the Vigil, kept as days of strict fasting, and by now, the forty days of Lent. We do not, however, have a Palm Sunday, a Maundy Thursday or a Good Friday, for the Vigil was the inclusive celebration of the one mystery of our redemption, which, though it had its two key moments in the death and resurrection of the Lord, constituted an unbreakable unity. It was only later in the fourth century that an historical sequence began to work itself into the paschal celebration; working forwards to the institution of Ascension Day and the transformation of Pentecost into a specific commemoration of the descent of the Spirit and backwards into the chronological observance of the events of the passion in Holy Week. This change in the character of Holy Week took place in Jerusalem and we shall have occasion to study it later. It is important, however, to grasp from the outset that this almost revolutionary new rememorative approach did not altogether obliterate the older unitive celebration of the whole mystery: the Easter Vigil retained its former character and even the liturgical texts for the new observances of Good Friday and Easter Day (the Day of the Resurrection) bore witness to a theological conviction that the Cross and the Resurrection form an indivisible unity and a single mystery. In the Middle Ages however this unity was obscured, and cross and resurrection became separated in theology, in devotion and in art with consequences that were to weigh heavily at the time of the Reformation.

One of the most conspicuous manifestations of this divorce was the Prayer of Consecration in the Communion Service of the Church of England's Book of Common Prayer, which concentrates exclusively on the passion and omits all references to the Resurrection.

From very early times the Paschal Vigil was associated with the rites of Christian initiation: the earliest clear references to this practice come from Tertullian in North Africa (in his *De Baptismo*) and Hippolytus of Rome (in *The Apostolic Tradition*) at the beginning of the third century, although Dr F.L.Cross has argued that 1 Peter represents a paschal baptismal liturgy.[13] By the time of Nicaea, at any rate, the Vigil had become *the* occasion for the reception of new members into the Church by what we are still accustomed to think of as the three distinct sacramental acts of Baptism, Confirmation and First Communion. The drawing together of the mystery of Christ's death and resurrection and of our identification with that mystery in baptism goes back at least to that famous passage from S.Paul's letter to the Romans which, since the latest reform of the Roman Rite, now forms the liturgical epistle of the Easter Vigil:

You cannot have forgotten that all of us, when we were baptized into Christ Jesus, were baptized into his death. So by our baptism into his death we were buried with him, so that as Christ was raised from the dead by the Father's glorious power, we too should begin living a new life. If we have been joined to him by dying a death like his, so we shall be by a resurrection like his; realizing that our former self was crucified with him, so that the self which belonged to sin should be destroyed and we should be freed from the slavery of sin. Someone who has died, of course, no longer has to answer for sin.

But we believe that, if we died with Christ, then we shall live with him too. We know that Christ has been raised from the dead and will never die again. Death has no power over him any more. For by dying, he is dead to sin once and for all, and now the life that he lives is life with God. In the same way, you must see yourselves as being dead to sin but alive for God in Christ Jesus. (Romans 6:3-11)

If Easter was the privileged and chosen occasion for the conferring of baptism, so the time before Easter was given over to the immediate preparation of the catechumens for their participation in the Easter mystery. A rigorous preparation was demanded of them and it was often a long one: three years were laid down as the norm in *The Apostolic Tradition* of Hippolytus of Rome. But a second stage of their preparation followed upon an examination of their conduct during the time of their catechumenate; those who satisfied this examination were now called the *electi*; and they had to undergo a season of more intense immediate preparation for their baptism, a time of instruction, prayer, fasting and exorcism. This solemn enrolment of the *electi* by the bishop took place at the time we would now call the beginning of Lent, and the season of Lent as we know it developed out of this season of discipline and final preparation of the catechumens for their initiation into the Christian mystery at Easter. Once more this use of Lent is becoming familiar - but only very recently, as far as our own country is concerned - to those Christian communities which have revived the adult catechumenate and adopted the new and extended Roman *Rite of Christian Initiation of Adults* (*RCIA*)[14].

We can easily understand how those who were already Christians came to feel that they could not be passive and indifferent spectators at the catechumens' time of final preparation but needed to manifest their solidarity with the candidates. Especially was this so since the Paschal Vigil involved them no less than the catechumens, and it was already recognized that it needed to be prepared for by a time of fasting. As early as the fourth century the evidence - as Dr A.A.McArthur argues[15] - makes it clear that "the church member was expected to approach the *Pascha* each year in the way he had done when he himself was solemnly preparing for his baptism."

It is important for us to understand the origins of Lent; to realize that it exists not only or primarily as a season of 'self-denial' but as a time for the intensification of the whole Christian life, a time of preparation leading to a climax. Like the monk in *The Rule of S.Benedict*, every Christian is called upon to keep Lent in such a way that he may look forward to the holy *Pascha* with the joy of spiritual longing – *cum spiritalis desiderii gaudio sanctum Pascha expectet*.[16] The catechumens were fasting, but they were also learning, as were the members of the community which sponsored them. At the end of the fourth century, the pilgrim Egeria describes the 'open' classes given in Jerusalem by the bishop during Lent for those to be baptized at the *Pascha*; – "any of the people who want to listen (the faithful, of course) can come in and sit down ..." So for every Christian Lent is a time for penetrating more deeply into the mysteries of the Faith; it is a time for learning. Indeed it is illuminating to see Lent as a corporate retreat for the whole Church, a refresher course on our baptismal vows of renunciation, faith and obedience[17]. In this perspective participation in the Easter Vigil – the centre, climax and highlight of the whole Christian year – will be regarded as little short of an imperative by the committed and instructed Christian. The Vigil from earliest times has had a strong baptismal reference, but in the conditions of the twentieth century the introduction into the rite of the solemn renewal of baptismal promises makes this unmistakably explicit, and must be counted one of the most brilliant and most profoundly pastoral of all modern liturgical innovations – or, perhaps better, renovations. This sense too of Lent leading to a joyfully awaited climax accounts for the paradoxical note of joy which was clearly expressed by S.Benedict. Witness is borne to this in more than one Christian tradition. In the Orthodox Church Lent is a season of 'bright sadness', a 'Lenten spring' whose arrival is to be greeted with joy , 'a time of gladness'.[18] In the new Roman Missal of Paul VI the first Preface of Lent gives thanks to God for "this joyful season when we prepare to celebrate the paschal mystery with heart and mind renewed." In the Anglican tradition the seventeenth-century parson-poet George Herbert can exclaim, "Welcome, deare Feast of Lent . . ."[19]

There is another feature of the ancient Lent that is important for our understanding of its meaning today, particularly for our understanding of the theme of penitence. A good starting point for our exploration is the rarely used Commination Service, provided for use on Ash Wednesday in the Book of Common Prayer. At the beginning of this rite the priest is ordered to read the following exhortation to the people:

> Brethren, in the primitive Church there was a godly discipline, that, at the beginning of Lent, such persons as stood convicted of notorious sin were put to open penance, and punished in this world, that their souls might be saved in the day of the Lord, and that others, admonished by their example, might be the more afraid to offend.
>
> Instead whereof, until the said discipline may be restored again (which is much to be wished) it is thought good that at this time (in the presence of you all) should be read the general sentences of God's cursing against impenitent sinners . . .

Lent was for a long time the period in which public penitents had to carry out the penances imposed upon them by the bishop, and it was at the beginning of Lent that they were enrolled in the order of penitents so that on Maundy Thursday (not normally of the same year, for the time of penance tended to be lengthy) they could be formally reconciled by the bishop and so share fully once more in the Easter eucharist. In the seventh century in Rome, Ash Wednesday was appointed for the opening of public penance and a dramatic rite devised for that purpose. Though it had long fallen into desuetude it was printed – along with archaic rites such as those for the blessing and imposition of a Crusader's cross; the handing over of degraded clerics to the tender care of the secular arm; the processional reception of the Holy Roman Emperor, and the reconciliation of penitents on Maundy Thursday – in editions of the *Pontificale Romanum* published up until the time of the Second Vatican Council. According to this rite the penitents are to prostrate themselves *cum lacrymis* (with tears) on the pavement of the church, and the bishop puts ashes on their foreheads saying, "Remember, man, you are dust and to dust you will return. Do penance and you will have eternal life." They are then clothed with sackcloth and prostrate themselves once more while the whole assembly recites the seven penitential psalms and the litanies. The bishop is then to preach (on Adam's expulsion from paradise), after which he leads the penitents to the doors of the church and ejects them *cum lacrymis*. As they kneel outside the bishop exhorts them "not to despair of the Lord's mercy but to devote themselves to fasting, to prayers, to pilgrimages, to almsgiving and to other good works, so that the Lord may lead them to the worthy fruit of true repentance." So the doors are solemnly closed and the bishop returns to the sanctuary to begin the mass.

We can imagine that this would have been a deeply impressive ceremony and would have had considerable impact on the whole congregation and not only the unfortunate penitents. All were to recite together the penitential psalms and we can see how – as in the case of the catechumens – the whole Christian people developed a strong sense of solidarity with the public sinners. Indeed, though we cannot after baptism become catechumens again, we can and must become penitents and remain so. With the development of Christian spirituality penitence came to be seen not just as a necessary activity after lapses into grave sin but as a positive and permanent Christian virtue. It was natural that as the discipline of public penance fell into disuse between the eighth and tenth centuries the Ash Wednesday rite should be transformed, and the whole congregation with the celebrant and his ministers receive the ashes of penitence. "Remember, man, you are dust and to dust you will return. Turn away from sin and be faithful to the gospel." This transformation was already widespread in 1091 when Pope Urban II added the full weight of his authority in extending this practice to the whole of western Christendom. So it was that Lent became a season of penitence for the whole Church militant.

*The Constitution on the Sacred Liturgy* of Vatican II summed this all up concisely:

> The two elements which are especially characteristic of Lent – the recalling of baptism or the preparation for it, and penance – should be given greater emphasis in the liturgy and in liturgical catechesis. It is by means of them that the Church prepares the faithful for the celebration of Easter, while they hear God's word more frequently and devote more time to prayer ...
>
> During Lent, penance should be not only internal and individual but also external and social. The practice of penance should be encouraged in ways suited to the present day, to different regions and to individual circumstances.[20]

This 'two-fold character' of Lent is also picked up and given clear expression in the new Order for the Beginning of Lent authorized for use in the Church of England in the collection *Lent, Holy Week, Easter – Services and Prayers* of 1986. This service is intended for use at the eucharist on Ash Wednesday, and indeed officially suggests the imposition of ashes for the first time in the Church of England since the Reformation, or it may be used optionally on the First Sunday of Lent. It is designed "not only to mark a special day but to start the local Christian congregation off on a path that can be seen, even at this early stage, to be leading to the Good Friday and Easter celebrations."[21] At the outset the celebrant is ordered to explain to the people the meaning of Lent and to invite them to observe it faithfully. He uses these (or other suitable) words:

> Brothers and sisters in Christ: since early days Christians have observed with great devotion the time of our Lord's passion and resurrection. It became the custom of the Church to prepare for this by a season of penitence and fasting.
>
> At first this season of Lent was observed by those who were preparing for Baptism at Easter and by those who were to be restored to the Church's fellowship from which they had been separated through sin. In

course of time the Church came to recognize that, by a careful keeping of these days, all Christians might take to heart the call to repentance and the assurance of forgiveness proclaimed in the gospel, and so grow in faith and in devotion to our Lord.

I invite you, therefore, in the name of the Church, to the observance of a holy Lent, by self-examination and repentance; by prayer, fasting, and self-denial; and by reading and meditating on God's holy word.[22]

Recognizing the feeling of solidarity with individual sinners felt by Christian people and wishing to stress even more strongly the ecclesial dimension of penance – the fact that sin has effects felt by the whole community and that the community has an important part to play in the reconciliation of sinners in its midst – the Roman Catholic Church introduced in its *Ordo Paenitentiae* of 1973 the idea of a public liturgy of penance. This service includes the reading of scripture and a homily, both of which are intended to prompt an examination of conscience; prayer; a general confession and in some circumstances absolution; the reconciliation of individual penitents in private, and a final thanksgiving. Obviously such services are particularly appropriate in Lent as the whole community prepares itself for full participation in the paschal mystery. This fact was clearly appreciated by the compilers of *Lent, Holy Week, Easter* which provides two entirely new penitential services for use in Lent (and, one supposes, at other times) in the Church of England. As one might expect, these take the form of corporate expressions of repentance in litany form and a general confession and absolution, but a form of absolution 'which may be used for the quieting of the individual conscience' is also provided. With the virtual disappearance of the Commination, with its fierce denunciations and the sort of anathematizing which is unsympathetic to modern ears, these services of penitence ought to reintroduce into Anglican lenten worship a dimension which has been sadly lacking.

At this juncture we are brought back to our starting point, the "forty days and forty nights" of the gospel for the first Sunday of Lent. The introduction of this narrative is not an irrelevant addition to the basic themes of Lent, distracting our attention from its real meaning and purpose. Rather, at the beginning of the old Lent (for at one time Lent began on this day), it sets before us our Lord's renunciation of the Devil and of the temptations of the world and the flesh which the Devil was seeking to exploit. Formerly this would have reminded the catechumens of the triple renunciation they had to prepare themselves to make at their Easter baptism: today it serves as a reminder to us that our baptismal renunciations, together with our profession of faith in Christ and our promise of obedience to God's will, need constantly to be reaffirmed, and that this is done in a particularly solemn and corporate fashion when we come to the end of our Lenten journey in the Paschal Vigil.

The element of renunciation, mortification and self-denial, an inescapable element in the Christian life, must always be seen in the context of the baptismal covenant and of the paschal mystery. Christians must never practise self-denial in order to assert the dominance of their wills over their bodies, for that cannot in itself bring us nearer to God; indeed, it may only increase our potentiality for evil. As Alexander Schmemann reminds us, "Christian asceticism is a fight, not *against* the body but *for* the body," and again, "In this world everything – even 'spirituality' can be demonic."[23] For Christians need to be very much on their guard against the heresy of the Manichees, which identifies evil with the material creation and seeks to release the spirit from the prison of the body: our Lord, on the other hand, told us that it is from the *heart* of man that proceed the evils that defile him. A great Anglican layman, poet and theologian, Charles Williams, who died in 1945, put this point very cogently when he wrote: "The body was holily created, is holily redeemed, and is to be holily raised from the dead. It is, in fact, for all our difficulties with it, less fallen, merely in itself, than the soul in which the quality of the will is held to reside; for it was a sin of the will which degraded us."[24] So we can see that no form of self-denial (so called) is of any value whatever – it can often be the reverse – if it is not directed to the love and service of God and our neighbour. Our model here must be Christ the Servant, laying aside his garments to wash the feet of his disciples. Our Lenten discipline must include a certain laying aside; we strip off our garments not because they are sinful but because they would hinder or limit our possibilities of service. It is a true instinct that has led to the recovery in our own days of the the ancient link between fasting and sharing one's food and one's resources with the hungry and underprivileged.[25] This link is clearly affirmed in the Old Testament and particularly in the passage from Isaiah 58 which is appointed in the eucharistic lectionary for the Friday and Saturday after Ash Wednesday. In the second century A.D. the following passage occurs in *The Shepherd of Hermas*:

> ... in that day on which you fast you shall taste nothing except bread and water, and you shall reckon the price of the expense for that day which you are going to keep, of the foods which you would have eaten, and you shall give it to a widow or an orphan or to someone destitute. . . .[26]

Finally, those who are familiar with the Divine Office of the Roman Rite will know part of a sermon by S.Peter Chrysologus – a fifth-century bishop of Ravenna – provided in the Office of Readings for Thursday in the third week of Lent:

> The fasting man should realise what fasting is. If anyone wants God to perceive that he is hungry, he should himself take notice of the hungry. If he desires fatherly kindness, he should display it first.[27]

So we are to say *no* to self only in order to be able to say *yes* to God and to our neighbour; to say *yes* more meaningfully and more authentically by attacking at the roots all the obstacles to our self-surrender. In our baptism we were called upon to say *no* to the Devil so that we might say *yes* to God: we were made to die with Christ to the old Adam so that we might rise with him to the glory of the new humanity. Our whole observance of Lent must help us to be conformed more closely to the death and resurrection of Christ in the Easter mystery. From the very beginning of Lent we need to have set before us the truth expressed so clearly by Louis Bouyer:

> The Pasch is not a mere commemoration: it is the cross and the empty tomb rendered actual. But it is no longer the Head who must stretch himself on the cross in order to rise from the tomb: it is his Body the Church, and of this Body we are members.[28]

## Notes

1. Alexander Schmemann, *Great Lent* (S.Vladimir's Seminary Press, N.Y. 1974) p.11.
2. *New English Hymnal* 67, (*English Hymnal* 73). Words by G.H.Smyttan and F.Pott.
3. Thomas J.Talley, *The Origins of the Liturgical Year* (Pueblo Publishing, N.Y., 1986) p.63 and 168, see also p.31. Talley argues that the 43rd canon of the Synod of Elvira in 300 AD is directed against the custom observed in some places of closing the Pasch-Pentecost period on the 40th rather than the 50th day, see p.62.
4. *The Festal Letters of S.Athanasius* (Oxford, 1854) p.21.
5. Talley, op.cit., p.169.
6. We say "sadly" not because we favour liturgical uniformity but because the Malta Report of the Anglican-Roman Catholic Joint Preparatory Commission in 1968 urged that "we should co-operate, and not take unilateral action, in any serious changes in the seasons and major holy days of the Christian year; and we should experiment together in the development of a common eucharistic lectionary." *ARCIC: The Final Report*, (London, 1982), p.112.
7. To many Anglicans the phrase *paschal mystery*, so familiar to Roman Catholics since Vatican II and the subsequent liturgical reforms, may seem strange and unfamiliar. It was, however, introduced into the *Alternative Service Book (1980)* for The Renewal of Baptismal Vows at Easter and retained in *Lent, Holy Week, Easter* (1986). The meaning of the phrase is further explored in Chapter V. cf pp.72-78.
8. *Vatican Council II, The Conciliar and Post Conciliar Documents* ed. Austin Flannery O.P. (Fowler Wright Books, Leominster, Herefords, 1975) para 106, pp.29-30.
9. A.A.McArthur, *The Evolution of the Christian Year*, (SCM, London, 1953), Part I : Sunday - The Basis of the Christian Year.
10. cf F.L.Cross, *1-Peter: A Paschal Liturgy* (Mowbray, London, 1954), and M.H.Shepherd: *The Paschal Liturgy and the Apocalypse* (Lutterworth, London, 1960).
11. Talley, op.cit., p.5.
12. Talley has argued that "while the discussion of the origins of the Christian Pasch seems sure to continue, the clear tendency of the recent literature is to recognize the Quartodeciman Pasch as the original form

of the observance, rather than as only a local variant of an annual
festival kept elsewhere on Sunday from the same period." *A Christian
Heortology* in *Concilium* 142 (2/1981) p.16. See also S.G.Hall, *The
Origins of Easter* in *Studia Patristica*, Vol.XV (Berlin, 1984) p.567.
13. F.L.Cross, op.cit.
14. At the time that this chapter was written, this exciting new development
    had hardly yet been experienced in England; we return to it briefly in our
    final chapter.
15. A.A.McArthur, op.cit., p.129.
16. *The Rule of S.Benedict in Latin and English with Notes*, ed T.Fry OSB
    (The Liturgical Press, Collegeville, Minnesota, 1981) Cap XLIX, p.253.
    A more accessible modern translation is provided in Dom David Parry
    OSB, *Households of God* (DLT, London, 1980) p.134.
17. John Wilkinson, *Egeria's Travels to the Holy Land* (Aris & Philips,
    Warminster, 1981) p.144.
18. Schmemann, op.cit., p.31 and p.43. See also Thomas Hopko, *The Lenten
    Spring* (S.Vladimir's Seminary Press, N.Y., 1983) passim.
19. From *The Temple*. For a good modern edition see the volume on George
    Herbert in *The Classics of Western Spirituality* (SPCK, London,
    1981) pp.204-206.
20. Flannery, op.cit. paras 109 and 110, p.30-31.
21. *Lent, Holy Week, Easter - Services and Prayers* (SPCK and others,
    London, 1986) p.12.
22. ibid. p.14-15.
23. Schmemann, op.cit., p.38 and p.84.
24. Charles Williams, *The Index of the Body* in *The Dublin Review* July
    1942. Reprinted in *The Image of the City & Other Essays* ed. A.Ridler,
    (OUP, 1958) p.85.
25. In *'Le jeune et la faim'* (a contribution to the symposium *Spiritualité
    Pascale*, Desclée de Brouwer, Paris, 1957), Michel Massenet argues that
    this link was clearly recognized in the first twelve centuries of the
    Church's history but then almost forgotten because of an unbalanced
    emphasis on the purely ascetic aspect of fasting at the expense of its
    social and charitable orientation.
26. *The Apostolic Fathers*, Vol.II, translated by Kirsopp Lake for the Loeb
    Classical Library (Heinemann, London, 1913) p.161.
27. *The Divine Office*, Vol.II (Collins, Dwyer, Talbot, 1974) p.155.
28. Louis Bouyer, *The Paschal Mystery* - English translation of the 2nd
    edition of 1947 of *Le Mystère Pascal* (Allen & Unwin, London, 1951)
    p.xiv. More recent French editions have been revised in the light of the
    liturgical changes of 1951 and 1955.

## Chapter II

# The Passover of the Jews

It is a pity that the English language has only a poor word like *Easter* to describe the centre and climax of the Christian Year. It is a word of Anglo-Saxon origin and its exact meaning is obscure; according to the Venerable Bede it is derived from *Eostre*, a goddess whose festival was celebrated at the vernal equinox.[1] Similarly, the word *Lent*, which is also of Anglo-Saxon origin, simply means Spring – the French has *Carême*, coming from the Latin *Quadragesima* meaning fortieth or a period of forty days. For Easter most European languages have words derived from the Latin and Greek *Pascha*, a version of the Hebrew word *Pesach* translated in our Old Testament as *Passover*; so in the French we have *Pâques* and in Italian *Pasqua*.[2] Instructed lay people may be familiar with the adjective *paschal* in such phrases as 'the paschal candle', 'the paschal vigil', and – more recently – 'the paschal mystery', but to talk of Easter as the *Pasch* is to invite derision or – more likely – blank incomprehension. Since in English we are obliged to accept this disadvantage of having to use two words – *Passover* and *Easter* – instead of one, it is not always as obvious to us as it should be that Easter is the Christian Passover.

The Old Testament narrative of the Exodus from Egypt features very prominently in the Lent and Holy Week liturgy. This background is given its most extended form in the Divine Office. The Office of Readings in the Roman Rite begins the reading of the Book of Exodus on the Thursday after Ash Wednesday and then continues from the Fourth Sunday of Lent with passages from Leviticus and Numbers. Then on the Fifth Sunday and until Easter the scripture readings are taken from the Letter to the Hebrews. The *Alternative Service Book* of the Church of England provides a two-year lectionary for use at Morning and Evening Prayer, beginning its cycle of readings on the Third Sunday before Lent. Genesis is begun on the following Monday and finished on the Saturday after the Fourth Sunday in Lent, and Exodus is begun on the Monday after the Fifth Sunday and continued (after a break in Holy Week) on Easter Monday. In the first year these lessons are read at Morning Prayer, in the second year at Evening Prayer.

It is not however only in the Divine Office that the Exodus story makes its appearance. Two key passages for the understanding of the Jewish Passover are Exodus 12, in which the Lord gives Moses and Aaron detailed instructions concerning the Passover meal, and Exodus 14, which describes how the people of Israel passed through the Red Sea on dry ground. The first of these two passages is now the first reading at the evening liturgy on Maundy Thursday in both the Roman and Anglican rites;[3] the second is the one Old Testament reading which must never be omitted at the Easter Vigil, and it may also be read at the Easter Day eucharist according to the *Alternative Service Book.*

Above all it is in the Easter Vigil that the reference to the Exodus story is at its strongest; not only or even primarily in the course of the Old Testament readings but even more vividly in the triumphal chant of the *Exsultet* or Paschal Proclamation.

This is our passover feast,
  when Christ, the true Lamb, is slain,
  whose blood consecrates the homes of all believers.

This is the night when first you saved our fathers:
  you freed the people of Israel from their slavery and
  led them dry-shod through the sea.

This is the night when the pillar of fire destroyed the
  darkness of sin!

This is the night when Christians everywhere,
   washed clean of sin
   and freed from all defilement,
   are restored to grace and grow together in holiness.

This is the night when Jesus Christ
   broke the chains of death
   and rose triumphant from the grave.

This magnificent lyrical hymn of praise was possibly
composed by the great fourth-century Bishop of Milan,
S.Ambrose, but its linking together of the Old Testament
passover story and the death and resurrection of Christ was
already traditional. In recent years there has come to light a
paschal homily, *On Pascha*, by Melito of Sardis, dating
probably from between 160 and 170 A.D. It proves
conclusively that the reading of the twelfth chapter of
Exodus was already a key element in the Christian paschal
celebration in the second century – at least in Asia Minor.
This is how it begins:

The scripture from the Hebrew Exodus has been read
and the words of the mystery have been plainly stated,
      how the sheep is sacrificed
      and how the people is saved
and how Pharaoh is scourged through the mystery.

Understand, therefore, beloved,
      how it is new and old,
      eternal and temporary,
      perishable and imperishable,
      mortal and immortal, this mystery of the Pascha:
old as regards the law,
      but new as regards the word;
temporary as regard the model,
      eternal because of the grace:
perishable because of the slaughter of the sheep,
      imperishable because of the life of the Lord;
mortal because of the burial in the earth,
      immortal because of the rising from the dead.[4]

Almost the only remaining vestige of this tradition to be preserved in the Book of Common Prayer, apart from the Easter Anthems, is the Proper Preface for Easter in which we give thanks for the glorious resurrection of Jesus Christ our Lord: "for he is the very Paschal Lamb, which was offered for us, and hath taken away the sin of the world; who by his death hath destroyed death, and by his rising to life again hath restored to us everlasting life." This was taken over from the old Roman rite, or rather its Sarum equivalent, and it is still preserved as the first Preface of Easter in the new Roman Missal of 1970.[5]

Some compensation for the comparative paucity of strictly 'paschal' material in the Prayer Book was provided for Anglicans in the nineteenth century by the translations of ancient Greek and Latin hymns by J.M.Neale and others. One fine example is the well-known Eastertide evening Office Hymn, *Ad cenam Agni providi*:

> The Lamb's high banquet we await
> In snow white robes of royal state,
> And now, the Red Sea's channel past,
> To Christ, our Prince, we sing at last.
>
> Upon the altar of the Cross
> His Body has redeemed our loss;
> And tasting of his precious Blood
> Our life is hid with Christ in God.
>
> That Paschal eve God's arm was bared,
> The devastating Angel spared;
> By strength of hand our hosts went free
> From Pharaoh's ruthless tyranny.
>
> Now Christ our Passover is slain,
> The Lamb of God that knows no stain;
> And he, the true unleavened Bread,
> Is truly our oblation made.[6]

If we try to look analytically at this rich profusion of liturgical material we shall find a triple pattern emerging.

First, the Passover of the Old Testament is treated in these liturgical texts as a *type* – a model, figure or prophetic image – of a fulness of redemption yet to come. Secondly, the Passion and Resurrection of our Lord are seen in terms of a passage – *Transitus* – and of a paschal sacrifice. Thirdly, our Christian life is also seen as a passage through death to life, or rather as a participation in the unique passing-over of Christ himself; in particular the passage of the Red Sea is seen as a type of Christian baptism. These are not so much three themes as three variations on a single theme; a single theme that is basic to our understanding of the meaning of Holy Week and the key which alone can unlock for us the complexities of the Holy Week liturgy. The introduction of this theme into the Paschal Liturgy is due to two developments. The first was the association of Baptism with the Easter Vigil (an association that is not made by Melito of Sardis but is first clearly stated, as we have seen, by Tertullian at the end of the 2nd century); the second was the influence of the 3rd-century Alexandrian biblical scholar and theologian, Origen, who challenged the faulty etymology of the Quartodecimans of Asia Minor, who had derived *Pascha* from the Greek word *paschein* (the present infinitive of *pascho*, to suffer)[7], and convincingly argued that its true meaning was *Transitus*, 'passage'. It was he too who applied this understanding of *Pascha* to Christ's passage into his eternal kingdom[8]. But these developments, far from deforming a primitive celebration of the 'event' of Christ's death and resurrection into a somewhat Platonic feast of an 'idea', in fact succeeded in giving explicit expression to a truth that is implicit both in the theology of S.Paul, who both referred to Christ as "our Passover" and spoke of Baptism in terms of identification with the death, burial and resurrection of Christ, and in that of the Fourth Gospel, in which the account of the Last Supper begins with the words, "Before the festival of the Passover, Jesus, knowing that his hour had come to *pass from this world to the Father* (our italics), having loved those who were his in the world, loved them to the end" (John 13:1).

The threefold Passover has known in its historical development some variation – Origen, for example, distinguishes between the Old Testament Passover, the Church's Passover and the Eternal Passover – but it always begins with the Old Testament, and it is here that we begin. First of all, a word of caution is perhaps necessary. Modern readers rightly feel uneasy with the idea of a type as a straightforward prediction or foreshadowing of a future event or person – undoubtedly one aspect of the pre-critical approach. But it is precisely the modern critical study of the New Testament which helps us to see how an author like S.Matthew felt free to shape his narrative round a retrospective reinterpretation of Old Testament prophetic material. As we grow to understand better the literary and theological impulses which shaped scripture, this reading back of Old Testament words and events in the light of the New Testament remains powerful and liturgically valid.

What are the main elements of the Passover story in the Old Testament? Israel, not yet a people or a nation but only a dispirited and unorganised rabble with no real sense of its identity, is in a condition of abject and helpless servitude under the iron grip of a ruthless and idol-worshipping Egypt. Moses – a fugitive from justice – receives a divine call and commission and to him is revealed the sacred name of the God of his fathers, *Yahweh*: "Now I am sending you to Pharaoh, for you to bring my people the Israelites out of Egypt." (Exodus 3:10) Things go from bad to worse: Moses is reluctant and timid, Pharaoh reacts with contemptuous anger – "Who is Yahweh for me to obey what he says and let Israel go? I know nothing of Yahweh." (Exodus 5:2) – and imposes an even heavier burden on the Hebrews, who turn in bitter resentment upon Moses and his brother Aaron. But there now follows a series of crippling plagues, bringing disaster on the the Egyptians and leaving the Hebrews untouched (Exodus 7,8,9 and 10). These plagues reach their climax in the death of all the firstborn of the Egyptians – the Israelites being spared through observing a sequence of new rites involving slaying a sacrificial lamb 'without blemish' (Exodus 12:5) and, after marking the doorposts and lintel of their houses with its blood, feeding upon it. Thereupon the Egyptians in desperate panic capitulate to the demands of the Hebrews and drive them out of their land in haste (Exodus 12:33).

Not for the first time Pharaoh changes his mind and pursues the Hebrews with the full might of his army, so that it seems that their darkest hour has come when they find themselves trapped between their pursuers and the waters of the Red Sea. At the last possible moment the waters are parted and the Hebrews escape, but as the Egyptian army follows them the waters return and overwhelm them (Exodus 14:5–31).

In the desert, the Hebrews are found to be fickle and faithless, but Yahweh travels with them, making his presence known to them in a pillar of cloud by day and a pillar of fire by night (Exodus 13:21), feeding them with manna and quenching their thirst with water from the rock (Exodus 16 & 17), as they journey through the wilderness towards the land which he has promised them, a land flowing with milk and honey. At the foot of Mount Sinai, Israel – a people now and no longer a rabble – accept the Law of God and enter into a covenant with the Lord who has redeemed them (Exodus 19, 20 & 24). God says "Now, if you are really prepared to obey me and keep my covenant, you, out of all peoples, will be my personal possession, for the whole world is mine. For me you shall be a kingdom of priests,a holy nation." (Exodus 19:5–6). This covenant is solemnly celebrated at the foot of Mount Sinai: sacrifices are offered and half the blood is thrown against the altar; then Moses reads the book of the covenant to the assembly of the people. They give their assent – "We shall do everything that Yahweh has said; we will obey." (Exodus 24:7); Moses then takes the rest of the blood and throws it upon the people, crying out, "This is the blood of the covenant which Yahweh has made with you, entailing all these stipulations." (Exodus 24:8). Yet the Israelites continue to rebel against God and to manifest their faithlessness, so that their entry into the promised land is delayed a whole generation. Moses dies, and it is Joshua, his lieutenant and successor, who leads the people across the

River Jordan (Deuteronomy 34, Joshua 1), in a way which is clearly intended to recall the earlier crossing of the Red Sea.

Reflection on the magnificent sweep of this story leads us to a number of conclusions. First, it should be noted that we are confronted here with the characteristic mode in which Scripture conveys to us the things concerning God and his relations with his people. Here is not doctrinal statement but *narrative* – story, from which first the Jews and then the Church, the believing community, has had to distil the truths it seems to require. As we shall see, it is pre-eminently through worship, through the liturgy, that we respond to this narrative, by participating in the story and by re-enacting it.[9] We cannot even begin to understand either the New Testamant itself or the Church's tradition of doctrine and worship until we recognise that they are set against the background of this particular story. This is most clearly true of everything that relates to the passion, death and resurrection of Christ and to the initiation of new members into the Body of Christ and the sacramental life of the Church. How else can we make sense of the references to the paschal lamb and the blood of the lamb, and to the 'sealing' of initiates with the sign of the cross (as the doorposts and lintels of the Israelites' houses were sealed with the blood of the paschal lamb)? How else can we make sense of the idea of baptism as a kind of passage through the Red Sea, and understand the words of S.Paul in his first Letter to the Corinthians (10:1-4)?

I want you to be quite certain, brothers, that our ancestors all had the cloud over them and all passed through the sea. In the cloud and in the sea they were all baptized into Moses; all ate the same spiritual food and all drank the same spiritual drink, since they drank from the spiritual rock which followed them, and that rock was Christ.

How else can we make sense of the idea of 'Covenant' – first offered to Noah (Genesis 9:9-17), to Abraham (Genesis 15:18), and then expounded in Exodus, but given its most profound development by the prophets Jeremiah and Ezekiel – and of our Lord's reference at the Last Supper to "the new covenant in my blood poured out for you" (Luke 22:20)? Yet at this stage, it could seem as if we have nothing more than a rather fanciful allegorization of the Old Testament, an arbitrary and artificial selection of random details and images.

We move on here to our second conclusion, that it is the Exodus story *as a whole* which points to the mystery of redemption *as a whole*, because it shows us the way God deals with his people. Our human predicament is one of servitude in the spiritual Egypt of sin, a servitude that leaves us weak and divided and incapable of initiative, for – as one of the old Lenten collects reminds us – "we have no power of ourselves to help ourselves".[10] Redemption can only come from the direct initiative and intervention of God himself, which is worked out in and through the history of a people. The lamb without blemish that is to be offered as a paschal sacrifice and consumed as a paschal meal, whose blood is shed to spare the firstborn of God's people from death, points to an awareness of the need for a pure and spotless victim who will offer himself as a vicarious sacrifice for the sins of his people and give them life through his death. The effect, moreover, of God's saving intervention is always to bind the redeemed into a close unity as the people of God and to establish a covenant relationship with them, not on the basis of human merit or as a bargain struck between equal partners, but on the basis of God's choice and calling, of his grace and his love.

In the passage from I Corinthians we have just been considering, S.Paul makes it clear that "all these things happened to them (that is the Israelites) by way of example, and they were described in writing to be a lesson for us, to whom it has fallen to live in the last days of the ages." (1 Corinthians 10:11). One strain in early Christian tradition tended to assert that the original Exodus was nothing but a type of what was to come, with no intrinsic value of its own. So Melito of Sardis in his paschal homily could argue:

The people then was a model by way of preliminary
   sketch,
and the law was the writing of a parable:
the gospel is the recounting and fulfilment of the law,
and the Church is the repository of the reality,
The model then was precious before the reality,
and the parable was marvellous before the interpretation;
that is, the people was precious before the Church
   arose,
and the law was marvellous before the gospel was
   elucidated.
But when the Church arose and the gospel took
   precedence the model was made void, conceding its
   power to the gospel.
and the law was fulfilled, conceding its power to the
   gospel.
In the same way as the model is made void, conceding
   the image to the truly real,
and the parable is fulfilled, being elucidated by the
   interpretation,
just so also the law was fulfilled when the gospel was
   elucidated,
and the people was made void when the Church arose;
and the model was abolished when the Lord was
   revealed,
and today, things once precious have become worth-
   less,
since the really precious things have been revealed.[11]

If, however, it is true that the most important thing about
the Exodus story is that it is a 'model' or 'preliminary
sketch' of the true redemption, yet it is also true, as S.Paul
affirms, that "God never adandoned his own people to
whom, ages ago, he had given recognition" and that "there
is no change of mind on God's part about the gifts he has
made or of his choice" (Romans 11:2 & 29). It follows that
we must also affirm that the Exodus event was a true and
valid experience of God's redeeming power for the people of
Israel. We need to recognize that it was a real act of God

and an integral part of his plan of redemption, and furthermore that both those who lived through it historically and those who have relived it liturgically in the annual Passover festival can in some sense be said to have eaten and drunk a supernatural sustenance, drinking from the rock that was Christ.

For the Jews the Exodus event constituted the central crisis of their history and their religion; it was a foundation experience, the event that gave them identity both as a nation and as the holy people of God. It is because the Christian Church is in direct continuity with this nation and people as "a chosen race, a kingdom of priests, a holy nation, a people to be a personal possession to sing the praises of God" (1 Peter 2:9) that we can sing in the *Exsultet* of the people of Israel as 'our fathers' and celebrate the Exodus event as part of our own history and our corporate experience of salvation. We can identify ourselves with the act of praise in the *Haggadah*[12] (the book which contains the liturgy of the *Seder* or Jewish Passover meal) when all raise their glasses and say:

> Therefore, let us rejoice
> At the wonder of our deliverance
>   From bondage to freedom,
>   From agony to joy,
>   From mourning to festivity,
>   From darkness to light,
>   From servitude to redemption.
> Before God let us ever sing a new song.[13]

If we do indeed have to go on to say that for the Christian this *Haggadah* finds its true fulfilment only in the *Exsultet* of the Christian Passover liturgy this is not to empty the Jewish Passover of all meaning but rather to give it a richer and heightened and universal significance.

Because the Exodus was so crucial to the Jews, the original core of history has been heavily overlaid with 'myth' - due to some extent to the annual re-enactment of the historical events in the dramatic and liturgical celebrations of the Passover festival[14]. We are in fact dealing with *Heilsgeschichte* - 'salvation-history' - in which historical events, their theological interpretation and their liturgical commemoration are bound inextricably together. Even the origins of the Passover are not free from obscurity; though it seems clear that two originally distinct festivals, probably earlier in date than the Exodus event itself, - a Feast of the Paschal Lamb with a pastoral origin and a Feast of Unleavened Bread with an agricultural origin - were at some time fused together as a single feast of the spring equinox and again at some time these Bedouin sacrificial customs were radically transformed, historicized and given their continuing legitimation by being related to the events of the Exodus narrative[15].

Furthermore, it is not even clear what the original meaning of the Hebrew word *Pesach* really was, for the later Jewish tradition differed over its interpretation. Josephus took it to mean the passage of the angel of the Lord over the dwellings of the Israelites at the slaughter of the Egyptian firstborn, while Philo took it to mean the passing-over of the Red Sea. The Old Vulgate accepted what is common to these two interpretations in its gloss on Exodus 12:11 - "*Est enim Phase (id est transitus) Domini*" - "It is the Passover (i.e. the Passage) of the Lord."

What is important for us to realize is the increasingly significant place the Passover came to fill in the life of the Jewish people. It was first of all 'eucharistic'; a great thanksgiving for deliverance and redemption, which came to include a commemoration of all the mighty deeds of the God of the Exodus in their history, some of which , like the deliverance from exile in Babylon, had already been seen by many of the prophets to fit into the same pattern. For example in Isaiah 48:20,21, and in Jeremiah 23:7,8, the promise of return from exile is clearly and explicitly modelled on the Exodus narrative. This process is still operative today when, for example, in a *kibbutz* in the modern State of Israel - the 'holocaust', the return to Israel and other events of recent history will also be recalled at the Passover meal. It was, secondly, a memorial of so intense and vivid a kind as to bring the past in some sense right into the present[16]. So in the *Haggadah* the leader says at a certain point:

In every generation, each person should feel as though he himself had gone forth from Egypt, as it is written: 'And you shall explain to your child on that day, it is because of what the Lord did for me when I, *myself*, went forth from Egypt...' Not only our ancestors alone did the Holy One redeem but *us* as well, along with them, as it is written: 'And he freed *us* from Egypt so as to take us and give us the land which he had sworn to our fathers'.[17]

These first two characteristics of the Passover have been admirably summarized by Rabbi Albert Friedlander:

Ritual is frozen theology which only comes to life when actual devotion and personal commitment by the worshipper turn the text and ceremony into a personal experience. 'I was brought out of Egypt', says the Jew on the first day; and many of us who came out of the much darker Egypt that was Nazi Germany say this with the deepest conviction and the most profound gratitude.[18]

For this reason the new introduction to the Offertory provided for the Maundy Thursday evening eucharist in *Lent, Holy Week, Easter* has deliberate echoes of the *Haggadah*[19].

It was, thirdly, intensely eschatological, since the Jews could not give thanks as they looked backward into their history without looking forward in prayerful longing and strong hope to a greater, more perfect and final act of liberation and redemption. Certainly in the time of our Lord there was always considerable excitement and unrest among the Jews at this season, so strong was the expectation of the Messiah's coming on Passover night, and the Roman Governor had to take special security precautions and make a point of always being in Jerusalem for the Feast. In the *Haggadah* today the eschatological note is strong, particularly as the meal draws to a close. The Cup of Elijah, which is set in the middle of the table, is filled with wine; the door is opened and the whole company rises, for, according to tradition, Elijah will come to announce and usher in the presence of the Messiah on Passover night. Shortly after comes the closing proclamation, which brings the formal part of the meal to its conclusion:

*Leader*: The Seder Service now concludes:
Its rites observed in full,
Its purposes revealed.

*Group*: This privilege we share will ever be renewed
Until God's plan is known in full.
His highest blessing sealed.

*Leader*: Peace!

*Group*: Peace for us! For everyone!

*Leader*: For all people, this our hope:

*Group*: Next year in Jerusalem!
Next year, may all be free![20]

It is easy to understand how even those Jews who have renounced or ceased to practise their religion can still be profoundly influenced by the Passover. So an agnostic Zionist can write:

What admirable teaching value there is in this recital of the enslavement of our people in Egypt and in their deliverance. I know of no other remembrance of the past which is so entirely turned towards the future as this memorial of the exodus from Egypt. How profound is the instinct of liberty in the heart of a people, if it has been able since its springtime to create this work of genius and transmit it from generation to generation ... This creation (the Passover Liturgy) has played a role it is impossible to neglect in the destiny of all the fighters and martyrs for liberty who have been raised up from the people of Israel.[21]

In reading this testimony it is difficult not to think of the role of the liturgy of Easter night in the Orthodox Church in Soviet Russia and of its power to sustain faith and to renew hope in the darkest circumstances.

The Christian Church must affirm with the greatest realism in its teaching and liturgy the positive value of all that led up to our redemption by Christ in the fullness of time. This involves giving full weight to the privileged witness of the Old Testament, for "salvation comes from the Jews" (John 4:22), but without ignoring the work of God in the rest of humanity. The words of Dame Maria Boulding, a Benedictine of Stanbrook Abbey, can help us to glimpse the wider perspective and perhaps even to be reconciled to our pagan word 'Easter':

> Christ died and rose in the spring, fulfilling the hope of the Jewish Passover feast which directly and primarily commemorated the exodus from Egypt. But behind the Passover stood ancient spring rituals, the sacrifice of spring lambs to ensure the fertility of the flock and the offering of the first sheaf of corn. Outside the chosen people the myths of death and rebirth were very powerful: the memories of the king who had to be sacrificed for the people, and the resurrection of the spring god as vegetation and crops were reborn after the death of winter. They were all vindicated in Christ's passover, those worshippers of Tamuz and Adonis and Osiris, the initiates of the mysteries that promised immortality, the Indo-Aryans who had rejoiced as Agni, their fire-god, sprang from the soft wood, and all those who through the ages had projected their hopes "into gods of unbearable beauty that broke the hearts of men". They are with us still, hiding in the shadows as we celebrate Easter night with the new fire and the water, the bread and the wine, because no fragment of truth, no gleam of beauty, no act of heroism or kindness or prayer can be finally lost.[22]

## Notes

1. Bede, *De Temporum Ratione*, I,v. An alternative explanation is given by Patrick Regan: "The English word Easter, like the German *Ostern*, comes ultimately from the old Teutonic *auferstehung*, meaning resurrection." "*The Three Days and the Forty Days*" in *Worship* 54,(1980), p.11, note 43.

2. The Hebrew *Pesach* is rendered in Aramaic *Pashka* – whence the Greek *Pascha*. The Old Vulgate introduced a complication since in the Old Testament it generally transliterated the Hebrew word as *Phase*, while using *Pascha* in the New Testament and in some Old Testament passages – e.g. Ezra 6:19-20; Ezekiel 45:21. The Douay-Rheims version uses both *Phase* and *Pasch*, following the Old Vulgate, but Mgr Knox's translation uses *Pasch* throughout. The New Vulgate of 1979 sticks to *Pascha*. The attempt of the Douay-Rheims translators to establish the word *Pasch* in the English language met with scant sympathy from the translators of the Authorized Version whose comment is distressingly polemical: "... we have shunned the obscurity of the Papists, in their *azymes, tunike, rational, holocausts, prepuce, pasch*, and a number of such like, whereof their late translation is full, and that of purpose to darken the sense, that since they must needs translate the Bible, yet by the language thereof, it may be kept from being understood."
3. Formerly in the Roman Rite it was read as the second lesson at the Good Friday liturgy.
4. Melito of Sardis: *On Pascha*, edited by S.G.Hall (OUP; 1979), p.3. Professor Hall in his introduction agrees that 'Melito may well have influenced the development of Christian liturgy'. He also refers to the arguments that *On Pascha* could represent an early form of the same genre that has given us the *Exsultet*, but without either accepting or refuting them (p.xxiv).
5. It has been preserved in both Rite A and Rite B in the *Alternative Service Book*, in spite of the savage mutilation it underwent in Series 3.
6. *NEH*, 101. (*EH*, 125) cf also hymns *NEH*, 104, 519, 106, 116, 117. (*EH* 128, 130, 131, 137.)
7. cf Melito, *On Pascha*, op.cit., p.46 "What is the Pascha? It gets its name from its characteristic: from suffer (*pathein*) comes suffering (*paschein*)."
8. *De Pascha*, cf Talley, op.cit., p.26.
9. see Anthony Harvey, *Attending to Scripture* in *Believing in the Church*, (Report by the Doctrine Commission of the Church of England, SPCK, 1981), pp.30-31. Also John Barton and John Halliburton, *Story and Liturgy*, pp.79-107 of the same collection.
10. Collect for the 2nd Sunday in Lent in the old Roman Missal and in the Book of Common Prayer.
11. Melito of Sardis, op.cit., pp.21-23.
12. The Hebrew word means 'narrative'. See Barton and Halliburton in *Believing in the Church*, op.cit., p. 106, note 2.
13. *A Passover Haggadah* - prepared by the Central Conference of American Rabbis, edited by Herbert Bronstein (Penguin Books, 1978), p.57. This passage leads immediately into the recitation of the first one or two of the *Hallel* psalms (Psalms 113-118); see also *The Passover, the Last Supper and the Eucharist*, (The Study Group for Christian Jewish Relations, London, 1975), and Chaim Raphael, *A Feast of History*, (Weidenfeld and Nicolson, London, 1972).
14. For a clear account of exactly what seems to be 'history' and what seems to be 'myth' see Siegfried Herrmann, *Israel in Egypt*, (Studies in Biblical Theology, Second Series, 27, SCM, 1973)
15. ibid. pp. 54-56.
16. So the 1971 Windsor Agreement on the Eucharist of ARCIC could comment: "The notion of *memorial* as understood in the passover

# 34 *The Passover of the Jews*

celebration at the time of Christ - i.e. the making effective in the present of an event in the past - has opened the way to a clearer understanding of the relationship between Christ's sacrifice and the eucharist." *ARCIC: The Final Report* (CTS/SPCK, London; 1982), p.14.

17. *A Passover Haggadah*, op.cit. pp. 56 and 57, quoting Exodus 13:8 and Deuteronomy 6:23.
18. Albert Friedlander, *Expressions of Joy and Gratitude.* in *The Times* (9th April, 1988).
19. President: At the eucharist we are with our crucified and risen Lord.
    We know that it was not only our ancestors,
    but we who were redeemed
    and brought forth from bondage to freedom,
    from mourning to feasting.
    We know that as he was with them in the upper room
    so our Lord is here with us now.
    All:    Until the kingdom of God comes
    let us celebrate this feast.
    *LHWE*, op.cit., pp.190-191.
20. *A Passover Haggadah*, op.cit. p.93.
21. Bert Katzenelson, quoted in *Pâque juive et chrétienne aujourd'hui* (Vérité, no. 25-26, Paris, 1970) p.5.
22. Maria Boulding, *Marked for Life: Prayer in the Easter Christ* (SPCK, London, 1979), pp.72 and 73 - quoting G.K.Chesterton: *The Ballad of the White Horse*, Book ii.

*Chapter III*

# The Passover of Christ

The basic theme of the Passover is that of a "movement from degradation to glory".[1] It is a journey to God, towards his Kingdom and the fulness of union with him; a movement that involves a pattern of deliverance from slavery through the shedding of blood; a movement that seems to end in the deep waters of destruction and death but which in God's mercy passes on through these waters to the Promised Land. We have seen that the Mosaic Exodus was both a real act of deliverance by God of his own chosen people and also a type, figure and prophecy of the central event in the history of salvation. It is this second aspect which we now have to explore, trying to understand how, in the light of the New Testament and the liturgy, the death and resurrection of Christ can be seen as his 'Passage' (*transitus*) to the Father and the fulfilment of the Old Testament Passover.

We must start with sayings which the Gospels attribute to our Lord himself. Most of those which concern us are concentrated in the last days of Holy Week and more particularly in the sayings at the Last Supper, but we have a few sayings of an earlier period that relate directly to our theme. In the predictions of his coming passion, death and resurrection Christ, on at least one occasion, makes special reference to Jerusalem:

Look, we are going up to Jerusalem, and everything that is written by the prophets about the Son of man is to come true. For he will be handed over to the gentiles and will be mocked, maltreated and spat upon and when they have scourged him they will put him to death; and on the third day he will rise again. (Luke 18:31–33.)

The explicit mention of Jerusalem is particularly significant in Luke, for whom the city plays a crucial role as the *locus* of God's action. It is found also in the parallel passage in Matthew (20:18–19) and in one of the Markan references (10:33), but it is Luke alone who records another saying:

for today and tomorrow and the next day I must go on, since it would not be right for a prophet to die outside Jerusalem. (Luke 13:33)

We need to remember that our Lord was making this journey to a particular place for a particular occasion – to celebrate the Passover in the holy city to which every devout Jew (until the destruction of the Temple and the termination of the Temple sacrifices in A.D.70) was expected to come for this festival.

Another important saying is given us by Mark immediately after the prediction of death and resurrection in Jerusalem: James and John, the sons of Zebedee, ask to sit at the right hand and the left hand of Jesus in his glory, and he replies:

You do not know what you are asking. Can you drink the cup that I shall drink, or be baptized with the baptism with which I shall be baptized?" They replied, "We can." Jesus said to them, "The cup that I shall drink you shall drink, and with the baptism with which I shall be baptized you shall be baptized. (Mark 10:35–40)

We need to compare this with another saying recorded by Luke:

I have come to bring fire to the earth, and how I wish it were blazing already! There is a baptism I must still receive, and what constraint I am under until it is completed! (Luke 12:49–50)

When Christ speaks in these texts of his baptism he is evidently not referring to his baptism by John the Baptist in the Jordan, for that is already behind him; he is speaking of his passion and death – and also of his resurrection. We are, as we have seen already, reasonably familiar with the idea of the passage of the Red Sea as a type of Christian baptism[2]; but is it too fanciful to see it here as a type of our Lord's death and resurrection, a passage through the waters of death to the right hand of the Father?

According to Hebrew cosmology in the biblical period, man lived in a 'three-decker universe' consisting of heaven, earth and the parts 'under the earth', and this last section was equated with the element of water. The sea was regarded as God's primordial enemy (Job 7:12), which it was his triumph to contain, and the deep waters are seen as the dwelling-place of monsters, Leviathan (Isaiah 27:1) and Rahab (Isaiah 51:9). Considered also as the abode of Satan and of Sheol, water is often used as a synonym of death or Sheol. This sign of water however is ambivalent; it can be both life-giving and death-dealing; it can bring salvation and destruction. The Old Testament is full of the imagery of the waters of death and of death by drowning, and this is particularly true of the Psalms:

Deep calls to deep in the roar of your waters:
    all your waves and breakers have gone over me.
    (42:9)

Save me O God:
    for the waters have come up even to my throat.
    (69:1)

Then the waters would have overwhelmed us
and the torrent gone over us:
    the raging waters would have gone clean over us
    (124:3)

It is also strikingly true of the Song of Jonah, a mosaic of Psalm-texts, which he prayed to Yahweh his God from the belly of the great fish:

Out of my distress I cried to Yahweh
   and he answered me,
from the belly of Sheol I cried out;
   you heard my voice!
For you threw me into the deep,
   into the heart of the seas,
and the floods closed round me.
All your waves and billows passed over me;
   then I thought, 'I am banished from your sight;
how shall I ever see your holy Temple again?'
The waters round me rose to my neck,
   the deep was closing round me,
   seaweed twining round my head.
To the roots of the mountains,
   I sank into the underworld,
   and its bars closed round me for ever.
But you raised my life from the Pit,
   Yahweh my God! (Jonah 2:3-7)

Matthew and Luke both record that Jesus rebuked his generation as an evil generation seeking for a sign, but "the only sign it will be given is the sign of the prophet Jonah." (Matthew 12:39 and Luke 11:29). They differ however in the interpretation of this sign which they attribute to Jesus himself; for Matthew it is the claim that:

For as Jonah remained in the belly of the sea-monster for three days and three nights, so will the Son of man be in the heart of the earth for three days and three nights. (Matthew 12:40)

but for Luke it is the preaching of repentance:

For just as Jonah became a sign for the people of Nineveh, so will the Son of man be a sign for this generation. (Luke 11:30)

However, if in this instance, Luke chooses an interpretation of the sign of Jonah that does not connect it with the paschal mystery of Christ's death and resurrection, it cannot be said that he is insensible to the importance of the Passover theme. In his account of the Transfiguration he records that Moses and Elijah appeared in glory and spoke to our Lord "of his passing which he was to accomplish in Jerusalem" (Luke 9:31). The Greek word translated *passing* is in fact *exodos* and it is clear that Luke has used this rather unusual word deliberately. S.H.Hooke has an interesting comment:

> Here one of the great recurrent images reaches its culmination and transformation in the experience of Jesus. We have seen Abraham's Exodus from Ur, the Exodus of Israel under Moses from Egypt, the Exodus of the remnant from Babylon, and the Exodus of the Servant of Yahweh by way of rejection and death from Israel's dream of national restoration. Now, from the Transfiguration onwards the final Exodus begins. We see Jesus with his face set towards Jerusalem, leading an uncomprehending and reluctant company of followers who were to be the new Israel carried with him through the waters of death, baptized with his baptism.[3]

So too when the Risen Christ, talking to the two disciples on the road to Emmaus, exclaims:

> 'You foolish men! So slow to believe all that the prophets have said! Was it not necessary that the Christ should suffer before entering into his glory?' Then, starting with Moses and going through all the prophets, he explained to them the passages throughout the scriptures that were about himself. (Luke 24:25-27)

The Passover theme may not be the only theme referred to here, but it is clearly one among them and one of the most prominent.

We turn now to the Last Supper and we find that all three Synoptists refer to it as the Passover meal. That this was in fact the case has been argued persuasively and with an impressive accumulation of evidence by the distinguished German scholar, Joachim Jeremias, in *The Eucharistic Words of Jesus*[4]. But Jeremias has not silenced all doubters[5]; one of the most recent of them, Thomas Talley, has reminded us that:

> while it has been easy at times past to dismiss this Johannine chronology (i.e. that the crucifixion oc- curred on 14 Nisan at the time of the slaying of the lambs for the Passover feast) as conscious theologizing of little historical merit, more recent exegetical opinion has been less inclined to reject the historicity of the Johannine chronology.[6]

This is not the place to sum up the arguments on either side and we would not consider ourselves qualified to attempt to judge between them. The Latin Church, in using unleav- ened bread for the eucharist, sided with the Synoptic interpretation; the Greek Church, in using leavened bread, sided with the Johannine. For the purposes of this study it is enough to quote the comment of Louis Bouyer on the whole controversy about the date of the Last Supper and on the efforts of modern scholars to resolve it:

> But all these arguments, however interesting they might be from the viewpoint of the Gospel story, are of no importance for the interpretation of the Last Supper and the eucharist to which it was to give rise. Actually, people are usually so concerned about them because they suppose the paschal references of the cross and the eucharist are all dependent upon the paschal character that may or may not be attributed to the Supper. Now this *a priori* is totally foreign to the reality. In the first place, the Passover setting is no less relevant to the Last Supper whether it preceded Passover (the immolation of the lambs coinciding in time with the death of the Saviour in this last case) or was actually the Passover meal. But - and this is of especial importance - the paschal references were pre- sent not only in the prayers of this one night but in all the meal prayers. And in fact, whether the Supper was this special meal or another, there is no doubt that Jesus did not connect the eucharistic institution of the new covenant to any of the details that are proper to

the Passover meal alone. The connection is solely with what the Passover meal had in common with every other meal: that is, the breaking of bread in the beginning and the rite of thanksgiving over the cup of wine mixed with water at the end. And, we may add, this is what made it possible for the Christian eucharist to be celebrated without any problem as often as one might wish and not only once a year.[7]

We are then on firm ground in asserting the paschal character of the Last Supper, whether or not it was actually the paschal meal, and of giving a paschal reference to the Words of Institution. The bread is designated by Christ as his body and it is the body of one who offers himself for his people, of one who is himself the paschal lamb. The Lamb is slain: the blood is already separated from the body and the cup is designated by Christ as his blood "poured out for many" (Mark 14:24). Moreover, there is a reference to the covenant in the words over the cup recorded by S.Paul and the Synoptists. This reference also is undoubtedly sacrificial, but its allusion is to a later episode in the Exodus narrative, to the sacrifice which ratified the covenant between God and Israel at the foot of Mount Sinai (Exodus 24:3-8). Then there is the command, recorded only by S.Paul but in what is in fact the earliest of the New Testament texts on the Last Supper, "Do this as a memorial of me" (1 Corinthians 11:25). If the Last Supper was the Passover meal then clearly the word 'memorial' has precisely the meaning it had for the Passover: "This day must be commemorated by you, and you must keep it as a feast in Yahweh's honour. You must keep it as a feast-day for all generations; this is a decree for all time." But the character of the eucharist as the Christian paschal memorial does not depend upon the Synoptic dating; it is not clear in any case that S.Paul adopted it[8]. The word *memorial* (in Hebrew, *zikkaron*; in Greek, *anamnesis*) has the same strong sense in other Jewish rabbinical and liturgical texts. As Louis Bouyer argues:

It in no way means a subjective, human psychological act of returning to the past, but an objective reality destined to make some thing or some one perpetually present before God and for God himself.[9]

In the Synoptic Gospels we find another reference by our Lord to the Passover in the narratives of the Last Supper:

When the time came he took his place at table, and the apostles with him. And he said to them, "I have ardently longed to eat this Passover with you before I suffer; because, I tell you, I shall not eat it before it is fulfilled in the kingdom of God." Then taking a cup, he gave thanks and said, "Take this and share it among you, because from now on, I tell you, I shall never again drink wine until the kingdom of God comes." (Luke 22:14-18).

According to Mark and Matthew this saying came at the end of the meal, and in a slightly different form:

In truth I tell you, I shall never drink wine any more until the day I drink the new wine in the kingdom of God. (Mark 14:25, cf Matthew 26:29).

According to the Lukan version – the most complex and difficult of the Synoptic narratives of the Last Supper – Christ spoke explicitly about the fulfilment of the Passover in the coming of the kingdom. Moreover in all three accounts the coming of the kingdom is seen in terms of the messianic banquet – eating and drinking in joyful communion with the Lord and his Anointed. But whereas in Mark and Matthew the coming of the kingdom seems to be set in a distant eschatological future, Luke gives a rather different interpretation. It is his Gospel which emphasizes the meals which the Risen Christ took with his disciples and which gives to them a eucharistic significance (Luke 24:28-32, 41-3; Acts 1:4; 10:41); his purpose clearly is to present the death and resurrection of Christ as in fact inaugurating the kingdom and fulfilling the Passover, and the Eucharist as the sign of the presence of the kingdom within the Church. As F.-X.Durrwell expresses it:

The Eucharist appears as the earthly anticipation of the feast to be celebrated in the joy of the new wine in the kingdom. The banquet in the kingdom is, in its turn, seen as a prolongation of the Eucharist, and is none other than the total fulfilment of the eucharistic supper; a 'perfected' Pasch at which we communicate in the true sacrifice of the Lamb.[10]

If we turn from the Synoptists to the Fourth Gospel we find at once the striking difference mentioned above – it seems indeed a direct contradiction – over the chronology of the Passion. According to John, the Last Supper was held on the night before the Passover and our Lord died at the very hour when the paschal lambs were being ritually slaughtered for the Feast. It is significant that at this point John notes that:

> all this happened to fulfil the words of scripture: "not one bone of his will be broken" (John 19:36).

The quotation comes from the regulations for the serving and eating of the paschal lamb in Exodus 12:46 and Numbers 9:12. As Michael Ramsey has pointed out:

> If S.John's dating is correct, this is a signal instance of his presentation of historical facts more accurately than the Synoptists. But if S.Mark's chronology is correct ... then we have a notable instance of S.John allowing theological symbolism to control the plan of his story: Jesus died as the true Passover lamb.[11]

Moreover it is in the Fourth Gospel that we are given sayings of Christ about his death and resurrection that express most clearly the idea of a passage (*transitus*) to the Father. Time and time again he links together the passion and resurrection in the one 'Hour' of his destiny: "The Father loves me, because I lay down my life in order to take it up again" (John 10:17). Later we are told that at the Last Supper, "Jesus, knowing that his hour had come to pass from this world to the Father, having loved those who were his in the world, loved them to the end" (John 13:1); that he repeatedly warned his disciples, "I am going to the Father. . . . I am leaving the world to go to the Father" (John 14:28; 16:28); and that in his final high-priestly prayer before setting out for Gethsemane he prayed, "Father, the hour has come: glorify your Son so that your Son may glorify you.... now I am coming to you" (John 17:1, 13). As Durrwell observes, 'Our Lord was not so much going *to* his death as *by way* of it: it was a mortal journey whose end was with the Father: "I go to the Father." '[12]

Earlier in the same work Durrwell succinctly indicates the wider paschal background of the whole of the Fourth Gospel:

> Knowing the subtle genius of this apostle, we can hardly think it coincidence that his gospel should unfold against the backcloth of the Exodus, that exemplar of the paschal mystery. The Word 'has set up his tabernacle amongst us' (1:14) just as God encamped among the Jews; Christ must be lifted up like the serpent (3:14); he has come down from heaven like manna, and will become our food (6:48ff); his followers will be refreshed by him as by the rock in the desert (7:37); they will follow him as the Israelites followed the pillar of fire (8:12). Christ is the paschal lamb (19:36). If this mention of the Exodus is to remind us of a very definite plan, then clearly S.John saw the paschal mystery of the Exodus as being repeated and perfected in the Word made flesh. He signposts his account by indicating the paschs that occurred during our Lord's public life (2:13,23; 6:4; 11:55; 12:1; 13:1). He does this so often that it imparts to the story a definite sense of direction.[13]

In fact, as the same author has pointed out more recently, the whole narrative of the Fourth Gospel can be seen as inserted between two proclamations of Christ as the Lamb of God and thereby defined - in virtue of the principle of "semitic inclusion" - as a "Paschal Gospel"[14]. At the very beginning of the narrative John the Baptist introduces Jesus to his audience and to us with the words, "Look, there is the Lamb of God that takes away the sins of the world" (John 1:19); and at the climax of the account of Christ's 'exaltation' we find a clear reference to the Paschal Lamb; "Not a bone of his will be broken" (John 19:36). Here, in one term – 'Lamb of God', the Evangelist gathers together significant allusions from a diversity of backgrounds but clearly focussing on the eucharistic practice of the Christian community for whom he wrote[15].

Our survey of the rest of the New Testament material must necessarily be brief. We have already noted in a previous chapter S.Paul's reference to the Exodus story for types of Christian baptism and eucharist; we need now to concentrate our attention on passages that refer to Christ as the paschal lamb. It is here that we need to exercise a certain caution, for when we are confronted with a passage like 1 Peter 1:18–19 – "For you know that the price of your ransom from the futile way of life handed down from your ancestors was paid, not in anything perishable like silver or gold, but in precious blood as of a blameless and spotless lamb, Christ", or with the many references to the Lamb in the Revelation to John (in chapters 5, 6, 7, 12, 13, 14, 15, 19, 21 and 22), we need to recognise that there is a whole wealth of Old Testament background to this image of the lamb and that the passover lamb is only one element among many. There is however one passage of S.Paul where the reference is explicit and unambiguous. "Your self-satisfaction is ill founded. Do you not realise that only a little yeast leavens the whole batch of dough? Throw out the old yeast so that you can be the fresh dough, unleavened as you are. For our Passover has been sacrificed, that is Christ; let us keep the feast, then, with none of the old yeast and no leavening of evil and wickedness, but only the unleavened bread of sincerity and truth." (1 Corinthians 5:6–8). Christ both fulfils the whole Passover story, transforming its meaning and significance for the Christian, and is also in his own person the paschal lamb. So in the *Exsultet* in the Easter Vigil liturgy, the deacon can proclaim, "For this is the Passover of that true Lamb of God, by whose blood the homes of all the faithful are hallowed and protected."[16]

One of the most powerful symbols of the Easter liturgy is the Paschal Candle and it bears eloquent witness to the Passover of Christ. It is of course a symbol of Christ himself, of Christ crucified and risen. At the beginning of the Easter Vigil the priest, should he choose to follow the traditional ceremonial, may mark the candle with a cross, with the letters Alpha and Omega, and with the date of the current year, saying: "Christ yesterday and today, the beginning and the end, all time belongs to him, and all the ages; to him be glory and power, through every age and for ever." He may then fix five grains of incense into the candle, saying: "By his holy and glorious wounds may Christ our Lord guard and keep us. Amen". The candle is then lit with the words: "May the light of Christ, rising in glory, dispel the darkness of our hearts and minds." All this should take place outside the main door of the church, with the people gathered about the fire that has been kindled there. Taking the lighted Paschal Candle, the deacon leads the procession of clergy and people into the empty and darkened church. Three times he solemnly raises the candle and chants, "The light of Christ!" or "Christ our light!" to which all reply "Thanks be to God." This new light, first piercing the darkness alone, is then passed from the Paschal Candle to the small candles held by the clergy and people.

The ceremony of this solemn entry looks back to the Exodus narrative, for it re-enacts the pilgrim procession of the Hebrews from the land of bondage through the Red Sea to the promised land, led by the pillar of cloud and of fire; in a few minutes time, in the course of the *Exsultet*, the deacon will proclaim: "This is the night when of old you saved our fathers, delivering the people of Israel from their slavery, and leading them dry-shod through the sea." The Roman rite adds, "This is the night when the pillar of fire destroyed the darkness of sin!" As the pillar of cloud and of fire was for the Hebrews a sign of the glory and the presence of Yahweh, so for us Christ is *the* Sign, *the* Sacrament, of God's presence and of God's glory. "The Word became flesh, he lived among us, and we saw his glory, the glory he has from the Father as only Son of the Father, full of grace and truth" (John 1:14). He is "the light of the world," "the real light that gives light to everyone" (John 8:12, 1:9). So also the symbol of light communicated from the paschal candle speaks to us both of the Resurrection itself (as in the collect of the Easter Vigil eucharist in the Roman rite: "Lord God, you have brightened this night with the radiance of the : isen Christ . . .,"), and also of the sacramental communication of the power of the Resurrection in baptism. Baptism is indeed an act of *illumination*, and we find the Greek word *photismos* used to describe baptism from the time of Justin Martyr in the second century. The author of the Letter to the Hebrews addresses the baptized as those who have been "brought into the light" and have "received the light" (Hebrews 6:4, 10:32), and in Ephesians we find a fragment of one of the earliest of all Christian hymns, almost certainly a baptismal hymn:

> *Wake up, sleeper, rise from the dead,*
> *and Christ will shine on you.* (Ephesians 5:14)[17]

When baptisms take place at the Easter Vigil, as indeed they should, then it is only after they have been baptized that the neophytes receive their own candles lit from the Paschal Candle. After Pentecost the Paschal Candle should be moved to the baptistry and used to light the baptismal candles throughout the rest of the year.

We can see how the Son of God would shine forth as the light of the world, guiding his people on their pilgrimage (John 8:12); we can see how he would feed and sustain them with heavenly manna (John 6:28-58) and with living water (John 4:13-14 and 7:37-39); we can see how he would be a new and greater Moses fulfilling the Law (one of the controlling themes of Matthew's Gospel, but see also John 1:17); and we can see how he would be a new and greater Joshua, effecting entrance to the promised land and place of rest, for the name Jesus is the Greek form of the Hebrew *Jehoshua* or *Joshua*, meaning 'Yahweh saves' (cf Hebrews 4:8). But the part that is most difficult to grasp is the assumption by our Lord of the role of the paschal lamb, suffering innocently and vicariously for our redemption. Why did he have to suffer in this way and why did God require it of him?

If the Incarnate Son of God had come into a world free from sin he could indeed have made his Passage, his *transitus*, back to the right hand of his Father without the cross and without the tomb. As the Eternal Son and Word he had eternally offered the perfect oblation of love and

homage to the Father, and his incarnation alone would have
sufficed to join humanity to himself and to draw the whole
created order into full association with his perfect sacrifice
of praise. Christ himself was without sin (Hebrews 4:15, 1
Peter 2:22); for himself he had no need to die. He came
however into a world that had torn itself away from God by
the violence of sin; he did not share the sin but he came to
bear the burden of it as the Lamb of God that carries the
sins of the world (John 1:29), and his acceptance of baptism
at the hands of John the Baptist was an act of identification
with sinful humanity in the grip of the powers of darkness.
Christ came into the world in order to return to the Father,
but not to return empty-handed. He came to bring
ransomed and liberated humanity with him (cf Mark
10:45). This involved a fierce and bitter warfare, because
the powers of darkness were not going to surrender their
hold on mankind without a struggle (Colossians 2:14-15;
Hebrews 2:14-15).

It is important to notice how often the liturgy of Holy
Week and Easter uses the language of combat. One thinks
first of all perhaps of Wipo's great, eleventh-century Easter
Sequence *Victimae Paschali*:

> Death and life have contended in that combat stupen-
> dous: The Prince of life, who died, reigns immortal.[18]

Then there are the two magnificent hymns by Venantius
Fortunatus, Bishop of Poitiers in the sixth century; *Vexilla
Regis*[19], used as the Office Hymn at Vespers throughout
Holy Week in the Roman Breviary, and *Pange Lingua*[20],
sung at the Office of Readings during Holy Week and, most
movingly, during the Veneration of the Cross on Good
Friday:

> Sing, my tongue, the glorious battle,
> Sing the ending of the fray,
> O'er the Cross, the victor's trophy,
> Sound the loud triumphant lay:
> Tell how Christ, the world's Redeemer,
> As a Victim won the day.

## Chapter IV

# The Passover of Christians

was because of God's love for us that Christ came into the
orld. From all eternity the love of God the Father had been
oured out in the Holy Spirit upon the Son and returned by
he Son in the Spirit to the Father. Christ took flesh in
rder that mankind might be incorporated into his human-
y and thus be carried up to the Father in the movement of
is love and the power of the Spirit. It is Christ "by whom,
nd with whom, and in whom"[1] we are enabled to
articipate in the eternal dynamic of self-giving love which
s the Holy Trinity. He came therefore into this world solely
n order that he might return to the Father, but return
bringing redeemed humanity with him. Because he came
nto a world of sin to unite to himself a humanity in the grip
of sin, we have already seen that his return could be no
peaceful journey, but a passover of mortal conflict with the
powers of darkness.

This passover struggle, brought to conclusion by our Lord
in his own person (for he was utterly alone as far as any
human support was concerned), was the unique and final
Passover in the sense that the work of redemption effected
by it has a final, once-for-all, finished quality. It is
unrepeatable,and yet it is constantly at work to effect our
own passover so that we may follow our Lord through his
passion and death to rise with him and sit with him and
reign with him. Yet this passover of ours is in no sense
independent of or distinct from Christ's passover; it is part
and parcel of it. The author of the Letter to the Ephesians
can speak of the action of God in raising Christ from the

Christ's warfare however was the warfare of love; he allowed
all the onslaughts of the powers of hatred and darkness to
be concentrated upon him; he accepted them without
resistance and without retaliation and still went on loving
those who tortured and reviled him. When evil had done its
very worst he still held fast, wavering not for a moment in
his faithful self-oblation to the Father and in his love for us:
and when he died evil could do no more to break the power
of his conquering and reconciling love. "It has been
fulfilled" (John 19:30), that is to say, "It is finished; it has
been accomplished."

We reject rightly all explanations of the mystery of the
Atonement which depict God the Father requiring to be
appeased by innocent blood before he can write off man's
debt and forgive him; we reject with horror any theology
which can talk of the Cross as 'the lightning conductor of
God's wrath.' We hold, nonetheless, that in the conditions
of this world of sin the Cross was necessary for our
redemption. In the Cross we see not God's wrath so much as
his infinite love. What we might interpret as God's wrath is
his valuation and condemnation of man's sin, which is so
hideous that it crucifies the Son of God. God cannot shrug
off our sin as a little matter of no importance: "Forgiveness
may be free but it is not cheap."[21]

We can never separate the Cross from the Resurrection
and we can never separate Christ's death and resurrection
from the recreation of humanity. It was necessary for there
to be a death in order that there might be a new beginning, a
new creation in the human race. As Durrwell puts it, "Our
Lord had become so completely one with the race of Adam
that what he wished to gain for us he first gained for
himself." And a little farther on he continues, "The
redemption of human nature is a drama unfolding first in
Christ."[22] We can say that Christ's death was a necessary
consequence of his acceptance of our fallen condition in his
Incarnation. Christ had to die because the Old Adam had to
die. Without death there could be no resurrection, no
glorification, no New Adam of the Risen Christ and his
Body the Church. Christ died not in order to exempt us
from dying but in order that we might die effectively and

really – in his death, and so rise to live effectively and really – in his resurrection.

Blessed be God the Father of our Lord Jesus Christ, who in his great mercy has given us a new birth into a living hope through the resurrection of Jesus Christ from the dead and into a heritage that can never be spoilt or soiled or fade away. It is reserved in heaven for you who are being kept safe by God's power through faith until the salvation which has been prepared is revealed at the final point of time. (1 Peter 1:3–5).

## Notes

1.   *A Passover Haggadah* (op.cit.), p.6 – from the Preface by Rabbi Herbert Bronstein.
2.   see above, Chapter II, p.22.
3.   S.H.Hooke, *Alpha and Omega* (Nisbet, Welwyn, 1961), p.181.
4.   The new English edition, translated by Norman Perrin and first published in 1966 (SCM, London), is based on the 3rd edition of the original German, with author's revisions up to 1964.
5.   cf. C.H.Dodd, *Historical Tradition in the Fourth Gospel*, (Cambridge, 1963) and A.M.Hunter, *According to John*, (1968). To these should be added X.Léon-Dufour, *Sharing the Eucharistic Bread* (Seuil, Paris, 1982, and E.T., Paulist Press, New York, 1987). We are grateful to the Reverend Paul Collins for this last reference.
6.   Talley, op.cit., pp.3 and 4.
7.   Louis Bouyer, *Eucharist, (Theology and Spirituality of the Eucharistic Prayer)*, trans. C.H.Quinn (University of Notre Dame Press, Indiana, 1968), p.99.
8.   cf. Talley, op.cit., p.4.
9.   Bouyer, op.cit., pp.103–104. Bouyer's interpretation represents an impressive consensus of scholars from very different traditions and is reflected in a number of recent ecumenical texts. It is, however, contested by some scholars in the Evangelical tradition, e.g. by R.T.Beckwith in *The Study of Liturgy*, (ed. Jones, Wainwright and Yarnold. SPCK, London, 1978), p.49.
10.  F.-X.Durrwell C.SS.R., *The Resurrection* (Sheed and Ward, London, 1960), p.57; cf. also pp.157–9, 323.
11.  A.M.Ramsey, *The Narratives of the Passion*, (Mowbray, London, 1962), p.21.
12.  Durrwell, op.cit., p.37.
13.  ibid., pp. 17–18.
14.  *La résurrection de Jésus, mystère de salut*, (Cerf, Paris, 1982), p.33. This is the 11th edition of a work originally published in 1950, and translated into English as *The Resurrection* in 1960. The more recent French editions are the result of substantial revision.
15.  J.Marsh, *The Gospel of St John* (Pelican New Test (Pelican, London, 1968) pp.123–124. C.K.Barrett, *to John*, 2nd Edn, (SPCK, London, 1978), p.176.
16.  This is the translation provided in *LHWE*; the Rom "This is our passover feast, when Christ, the true L blood consecrates the homes of all believers."
17.  This hymn is put into the mouth of the celebrant as t the Paschal Vigil in the liturgy of the Taizé Comm *Pascales à Taizé* (Taizé, 1971), p.70.
18.  *NEH* Hymn 519. (*EH* 130).
19.  *NEH* Hymn 79. (*EH* 94).
20.  *NEH* Hymn 78. (*EH* 95).
21.  Fr Hugh S.S.F., *No Escape from Love*, (Faith Press, Lo
22.  Durrwell, *The Resurrection*, op.cit., pp.56, 58.

dead and his action in raising us up to newness of life as one
single movement, as one single action:

> But God, being rich in faithful love, through the great
> love with which he loved us, even when we were dead in
> our sins, brought us to life with Christ – it is through
> grace that you have been saved – and raised us up with
> him and gave us a place with him in heaven, in Christ
> Jesus (Ephesians 2:4–6).

To understand this identification we need to return once
more to what S.Paul says about baptism in the Epistle to
the Romans.

> You cannot have forgotten that all of us, when we
> were baptized into Christ Jesus, were baptized into his
> death. So by our baptism into his death we were buried
> with him, so that as Christ was raised from the dead by
> the Father's glorious power, we too should begin living
> a new life. If we have been joined to him by dying a
> death like his, so we shall be by a resurrection like his;
> realising that our former self was crucified with him, so
> that the self which belonged to sin should be destroyed
> and we should be freed from the slavery of sin.
> Someone who has died, of course, no longer has to
> answer for sin.
>
> But we believe that, if we died with Christ, then we
> shall live with him too. We know that Christ has been
> raised from the dead and will never die again. Death
> has no power over him any more. For by dying, he is
> dead to sin once and for all, and now the life that he
> lives is life with God. In the same way, you must see
> yourselves as being dead to sin but alive for God in
> Christ Jesus. (Romans 6:3–11)

It is in this passage more clearly than anywhere else in
the New Testament that we are confronted with the
identification of the Christian with Christ precisely in the
act of his passover – his *transitus* – by the way of the Cross
to the glory of the Resurrection. It is on the paschal
character of Christian baptism that this view of the
Christian life as passover is founded.

Whatever variations there may have been in early baptismal practice, it is clear that in this passage S.Paul's language is inspired by the symbolism of immersion. The etymological meaning of 'baptize' is 'dip', hence the sinner's immersion in water can be seen as a symbolic death and burial. While elsewhere, notably in 1 Cor 6:11 and Titus 3:5, Paul or his pseudonymous disciple speaks of baptism in terms of a cleansing bath, here the function of the water is not so much to wash as to drown. Baptism, in the vivid phrase of Norman Nicholson, is "birth by drowning"[2] and thus recalls the story of Noah and the Flood, the experience of the Israelites at the Red Sea, and the Exodus which our Lord had to accomplish at Jerusalem and which he spoke of as his baptism (Luke 12:50). So it is that the First Letter of Peter can speak of the ark of Noah as an antitype of baptism (1 Peter 3:20–21) and S.Paul can speak thus of the Israelites, "In the cloud and in the sea they were all baptized into Moses" (1 Cor 10:2). The baptism service in the Book of Common Prayer includes a prayer which after mentioning Noah, speaks of God's leading the children of Israel through the Red Sea, "figuring thereby thy holy Baptism." In the new Roman Rite of Baptism the prayer for the blessing of baptismal water is rich in typological allusion; the Flood, the Red Sea and the stream of water from our Lord's side as he hung upon the Cross are all mentioned[3]. The *ASB* baptism service makes allusion to the waters of the Red Sea in the thanksgiving prayer over the water of baptism but omits the explicit typological reference[4]. The context makes clear that, in addition to bringing new life, water can also bring death by drowning, and the themes of life and death and their paradoxical relationship are given true significance in the baptism, death and resurrection of Jesus Christ[5].

The link between baptism and the death and resurrection of our Lord was made strikingly explicit in the developed ceremonial of the Early Church. The rites of baptism were truly awe-inspiring and the operative symbolism had an immediacy and an impact which it is hard to recapture today. The candidates descended to the font in semi-darkness, stripped off all their clothes and were anointed all over with oil to prepare them, like athletes, for their struggle with the Devil. Facing west to renounce the Devil and all his works, they were immersed three times in the waters.[6] They then ascended from the font towards the east, were anointed on the forehead (sealed with the Holy Spirit), clothed in white robes and given lighted candles. Thus dressed and carrying their candles they entered the church to participate for the first time in the whole of the Eucharist and to receive Communion. When receiving Communion they partook of three chalices; the chalice of wine – of course, but also a chalice of water to signify the washing of the inner man, and a chalice of milk and honey mixed to celebrate their entry into the 'Promised Land'. All this moreover took place, if possible, in the night of Easter: the catechumens celebrated their own death and resurrection in the celebration of Christ's death and resurrection.

The distinctively Pauline death-resurrection imagery of baptism is not concerned with a merely symbolic act; he speaks of the Christian's real identification with our Lord's death and resurrection. Christ's death marked the moment of his victory over the powers of evil; death could no longer have any dominion over him, for he was at this moment freed from all the limitations and humiliations imposed upon him by his identification of himself with our humanity in its fallen state. Death was for him the gateway to his glorification. So too our identification in baptism with the death of Christ is not an identification with the physical act of disintegration but with the act in which our Lord renounced and triumphed over the old Adam, liberating the human race from the grip of the powers of sin and death. And as our identification with his death is not a literal anticipation of the moment of our own physical death, neither is our identification with his resurrection a literal anticipation of the moment of our bodily resurrection, but an identification with his resurrection as the creative act by which God renewed the human race in exalting and glorifying his Son and in pouring out his Holy Spirit. The baptism of Christ by John the Baptist was undoubtedly the determining historical influence upon Christian baptism and the Gospel accounts of Christ's baptism were probably affected by the liturgical traditions of the earliest Christian congregations. From the account in Mark 1:9–11 and its parallels in Matthew and Luke it seems clear that Christ's baptism was associated with divine sonship. It would thus seem reasonable to conclude that for S.Paul men could be spoken of as "becoming sons of God" in Baptism. If S.Paul can quote Psalm 2: "You are my son: today I have fathered you" as a reference to the Resurrection (Acts 13:33), so there is a sense in which we can apply it to ourselves as a reference to our baptism.

However, if we confine ourselves to seeing our own passover in terms of baptism alone we shall never make sense of it. Baptism is but a part, if the most important part, of a unified movement of Christian Initiation which, as the description of early baptismal ceremonies given above has already hinted, also includes Confirmation and First Communion. The General Introduction to the revised rites of Christian Initiation in the new Roman Ritual expresses it thus;

> Through the sacraments of Christian initiation men and women are freed from the power of darkness. With Christ they die, are buried and rise again. They receive the Spirit of adoption which makes them God's sons and daughters and, with the entire people of God, they celebrate the memorial of the Lord's death and resurrection.[7]

The movement from darkness to light acted out in the baptistry is a real removal or change effected by God. S.Paul tells us that God has "rescued us from the ruling force of darkness and transferred us to the kingdom of the Son that he loves, and in him we enjoy our freedom, the forgiveness of sin" (Col 1:13–14). Every other aspect of baptismal grace – forgiveness, regeneration, the conferring of character – must be seen in the light of this movement in which we are so completely identified with Christ as to be incorporated into the body of his risen and glorified humanity, identified with him moreover in his own passage through darkness to light, in his death and resurrection. As our own experience demonstrates, it is not that our baptism places us immediately into a state of perfection and easy security where we have no need to fight and no risk of falling. Rather, in baptism we are united with Christ so that in the victorious power and energy of his risen life we may be transformed and continually live out our baptism by being conformed to him in his warfare against evil and in his death to sin.

When the neophytes emerged from the waters of the font they were anointed again and received the laying on of hands, a rite which in a later form and detached from its Easter context we have come to know as Confirmation. It is difficult to appreciate the paschal character of Confirmation when it is celebrated in isolation, detached from Baptism, but when, as is increasingly the case, the sacraments of initiation are linked together in a single rite there seems to be a progression from the strictly paschal character of Baptism (incorporation into Christ's death, burial and resurrection) to the more pentecostal character of Confirmation (bestowal of the gifts of the Spirit). S.Augustine saw it as all part and parcel of the same process, "When you were exorcised, it was the grinding of you. When you were baptized, it was your moistening. When you received the fire of the Holy Spirit, it was the baking of you."[8] This is not the place to teaze out the relationship of Baptism to Confirmation but, as the Lima Report – *Baptism, Eucharist and Ministry* – puts it,

> In God's work of salvation, the paschal mystery of Christ's death and resurrection is inseparably linked with the pentecostal gift of the Holy Spirit. Similarly, participation in Christ's death and resurrection is inseparably linked with the receiving of the Spirit. Baptism in its full meaning signifies and effects both.[9]

It may be helpful in this context to remember that what S.Luke sees as two moments, Easter and Pentecost, the Fourth Gospel brings together as a single event – Easter Day. As we shall see in a later chapter, *Pascha* and Pentecost form a single unity.

Baptized, sealed with the Spirit and robed in white, the new Christians entered the church proper to participate in the Eucharist and receive Holy Communion for the first time.

> The Lamb's high banquet we await
> In snow-white robes of royal state;
> And now the Red Sea's channel past,
> To Christ, our Prince, we sing at last.[10]

The Fourth Gospel records that while the dead Christ hung on the Cross on Calvary, "one of the soldiers pierced his side with a lance; and immediately there came out blood and water" (John 19:34). This remarkable incident is Johannine material without parallel in the Synoptic accounts of the Passion[11]. As the strong following verse indicates, it must have had very great significance for the Evangelist or his immediate redactors. An allusion to the two sacraments of Baptism and Eucharist is so immediately apparent that many commentators have felt it necessary to devote much energy to the attempt to prove that such an interpretation is inadmissible[12]. Nevertheless, Patristic exegetes of the text worked under no such inhibition and from Tertullian on there is a strong tradition of seeing the wound in Christ's side as the birthplace of the Church and the source of the efficacy of the sacraments[13]. S.John Chrysostom makes the point with some force in his Homilies on S.John's Gospel. Commenting on John 19:34 he observes:

> With this too an ineffable mystery was accomplished. For there came forth water and blood. Not without a purpose, or by chance, did these two founts come forth, but because by means of these two together the Church consisteth. and the initiated know it, being by water indeed regenerate, and nourished by the Blood and the Flesh. Hence the Mysteries (sacraments) take their beginning; that when thou approachest to that aweful cup, thou mayest so approach, as drinking from the very Side.[14]

Whether John himself intended this construction to be put upon his words remains the subject of scholarly debate, but it is interesting that Oscar Cullmann maintains that this text represents a climax in the gospel and contains the key to the understanding of John's whole purpose; that of setting forth the connection between contemporary Christian worship and the historical life of Jesus[15]. John records that Jesus himself spoke of his body as a Temple (John 2:19–22) and, echoing Isaiah (44:3), cried out, "Let anyone who is thirsty come to me! Let anyone who believes in me come and drink! As scripture says, 'From his heart shall flow streams of living water.' " (John 7:37–8) In most artistic representations of Christ crucified, the wound inflicted by the soldier's lance is shown on the right hand side of the body, even though basic anatomy teaches us that the heart is on the left. The Church's liturgical meditation on and transmission of Scripture has here influenced the development of iconography, as one would hope and expect it should, the underlying notion being the fulfilment of the prophecy of Ezekiel in the Passion of Christ:

> He brought me back to the entrance of the Temple, where a stream flowed eastwards from under the Temple threshold, for the Temple faced east. The water flowed from under the *right* side of the Temple . . . the water flowed out on the *right-hand* side . . . wherever the river flows all living things teeming in it will live . . . . wherever the water goes it brings health, and life teems wherever the river flows. (Ezekiel 47:1–2,9)

The rich image is taken up again in Johannine literature, in Revelation 22:1–2, where the river of life is seen "rising from the throne of God and of the Lamb". All this finds appropriate liturgical expression when the rite of sprinkling the congregation with holy water is performed at the beginning of the Sunday eucharist in Eastertide with the traditional chant *Vidi Aquam*, "I saw water flowing from the right side of the temple, alleluia. It brought God's life and his salvation, and the people sang in joyful praise: alleluia, alleluia."[16]

The patristic exegesis of John 19:34 points us to the truth that Baptism and Eucharist both unite us to the mystery of the Cross. For if we are united once for all to Christ in his

death and resurrection by being grafted through Baptism
into his body the Church, this union is kept in being and
constantly renewed and strengthened by the Eucharist
wherein he commanded his disciples to remember and
encounter him, as the continuing people of God, until his
return. The Eucharist no less than Baptism is a paschal
sacrament, for as "the new paschal meal of the Church,"[17]
the new passover banquet, it is the sacrament of the unity
of the Body of Christ with its glorified and ascended head,
the memorial of the Cross and Resurrection, the sacrifice of
praise. As a sacrifice it is in no sense independent of or
additional to that of Calvary; it is identical with it, for as an
*anamnesis* of the historical event it exists to bring us into
vital contact with the once for all event of Christ's death
and resurrection. And no less than Baptism and Confirmation is the Eucharist a pentecostal sacrament for it is the
Holy Spirit "who makes the crucified and risen Christ
really present to us in the eucharistic meal" and "who
makes the historical words of Jesus present and alive." [18]

If we consider the significance of what our Lord did and
said over the bread and wine on the night before he
suffered, we shall see that first of all he plainly declared his
coming death to be a sacrifice, with his body being given
and his blood being poured out for the forgiveness of sins
and for the inauguration of a new covenant, a radically new
kind of relationship between God and man. By his words
and actions he not only declared his death to be a sacrifice;
he also solemnly consecrated himself to that sacrifice,
acting both as Priest and as Victim. But our Lord went one
step further, for he gave the Bread and the Cup to his
disciples, commanding them to eat and to drink. By this he
was drawing his disciples into the closest association with
his sacrifice; for by continuing to "do this" through the ages
they were not only communicating in the fruits of his
oblation but in the very act of oblation itself.

If we ask who it is that offers in the eucharistic sacrifice
we do not have to make a choice between saying either that
it is Christ or that it is the Church; similarly if we ask who
or what it is that is offered in the eucharistic sacrifice we do
not have to choose between Christ and his Church. The

Eucharist is precisely the sacrament of unity, of the unity of Head and members in one Body; it is the sacrament of the whole Christ, *Totus Christus*.[19] In the Eucharist it is the whole Christ that offers and the whole Christ that is offered, for it is the means whereby the barriers of time and space are transcended and Christ's members in every place and in every generation "enter into the movement of his self-offering."[20] At every Eucharistic celebration we give ourselves to be laid upon the altar in our gifts of bread and wine and to be offered in and with our gifts in sacrifice and thanksgiving to the Father; we give our lives for Christ to say over them, as over our gifts, "This is my body . . . This is my blood"; we give our lives to be broken, and shared, and given away. Both in consecration and in communion our lives are identified with the life of Christ and our offering of ourselves with Christ's offering of himself.

The Eucharist is thus the supreme link between Christ's sacrifice and the present life of the Church – between his *transitus* and our own. The Church has nothing of her own to offer but the offering of Christ made once for all upon the Cross and accepted and vindicated in the Resurrection, and so she only dares to offer herself in and through her Head and Bridegroom and his perfected and unspotted sacrifice. As the *Final Report* of ARCIC puts it:

> On the one hand, the eucharistic gift springs out of the Paschal Mystery of Christ's death and resurrection, in which God's saving purpose has already been definitively realized. On the other hand, its purpose is to transmit the life of the crucified and risen Christ to his body, the Church, so that its members may be more fully united to Christ and to one another.[21]

So then a paschal character is given not only to our baptism but to our eucharistic worship and through that to our whole Christian life. Death too, for the Christian, has a paschal character. "Physical death consummates sacramental death; it completes our incorporation into Christ in his redemptive act. The summit, as it were, of man's carnal weakness becomes, in his acceptance of it, the supreme means of being caught up with the Saviour in his death and

therefore also in his triumph."[22] We can understand
therefore, why *The Constitution on the Sacred Liturgy* of
Vatican II could decide that "funeral rites should express
more clearly the paschal character of Christian death."[23]
This decree has in fact determined the revision of the
funeral rites of the Roman rite, so that now most of the
heavy and lugubrious texts of the later Middle Ages have
been removed and a note of paschal joy and hope
reintroduced[24]. Visually too there is a change; while black
remains an optional liturgical colour it has generally been
replaced by purple or white, and it is recommended that the
Paschal Candle should be lit and placed at the head of the
coffin. This same spirit has been at work in Anglican
revisions – though much more clearly in the new American
than the new English rite.[25] *Lent, Holy Week, Easter* allows
for the Paschal Candle, moved to a place near the font after
Pentecost and used at Baptisms throughout the year, to be
used also at funerals.[26]

It is significant that S.Paul constantly writes of Christian
living and dying not in terms of the Cross alone, nor in
terms of the Resurrection alone, but in terms of both united
together.

> For him (Christ) I have accepted the loss of all other
> things, and look on them all as filth if only I can gain
> Christ and be given a place in him, with the upright-
> ness I have gained not from the Law, but through faith
> in Christ, an uprightness from God, based on faith,
> that I may come to know him and the power of his
> resurrection, and partake of his sufferings by being
> moulded to the pattern of his death, striving towards
> the goal of resurrection from the dead (Phil 3:8-11).

In these verses we see put in a nutshell the essential
character of Christian living: it is knowing the fellowship of
Christ's sufferings and the power of his resurrection. Again
S.Paul tells us that

> we are children of God. And if we are children, then we
> are heirs, heirs of God and joint heirs with Christ,

provided that we share his suffering, so as to share his
glory (Rom 8:16-17);

and earlier in the same epistle he refers to Christ as

our Lord Jesus who was handed over to death for our
sins and raised to life for our justification (Rom
4:24-25).

There is a sense in which it can be said that we are still
waiting for the final and definitive Passover, which is the
*Parousia*, the return of Christ in power and glory. But if for
the Jews in the Old Testament the true reality of the
Passover was all in the future, it is not so for us: we look
back to the central act of history, no mere type or figure but
the true substance of our redemption, and we look forward
to our resurrection not as something set totally in the future
but as something begun in us at our baptism. The new life,
the new age of the Spirit, has already begun; so we "throw
out the old yeast" (1 Cor 5:7) that we may celebrate the
Passover of Unleavened Bread in newness of life. That the
new life has already begun, that our translation has already
been effected, is the message of one of the readings for the
Mass of Easter Day:

Since you have been brought back to true life with
Christ, you must look for the things that are in heaven,
where Christ is, sitting at God's right hand. Let your
thoughts be on heavenly things, not on the things that
are on the earth, because you have died, and now the
life you have is hidden with Christ in God. But when
Christ is revealed - and he is your life - you too will be
revealed in all your glory with him (Col 3:1-4).

The process of our sanctification is nothing else than the
transformation and transfiguration of our lives by the
paschal light of Christ. "And all of us," says S.Paul, "with
our unveiled faces like mirrors reflecting the glory of the
Lord, are being transformed into the image that we reflect
in brighter and brighter glory" (2 Cor 3:18); "My dear
friends," says S.John, "we are already God's children, but

what we shall be in the future has not yet been revealed. We are well aware that when he appears we shall be like him, because we shall see him as he really is" (1 John 3:2). A moving contemporary statement of this understanding of the process of sanctification in the light of the Paschal Mystery has been made by Dame Maria Boulding:

> The bafflement and sense of failure that we go through all the time, in prayer and in the whole of life, are our insertion into his experience. In our blundering and disillusionment, our failure and weakness and inconsistencies, he is living out again his own Easter passage to perfect obedience, his own long-matured act of surrender into the Father's hands. If this is true – and I am more and more convinced that it is – then the Easter glory cannot be entirely some deferred thing; it must be present now as the secret meaning of a great deal of our daily experience. The signs of the new creation are already with us and we know, intermittently and obscurely, the wholeness that is to come.[27]

The Holy Week liturgy is concerned, as we have seen, with the Passover of the Jews and with the Passover of Christ. It is no less concerned with *our* Passover, and it is engaged in the work of effecting it through the ministry of the Word and of the Sacraments. "Cross and resurrection," wrote Michael Ramsey, "are the grounds of the Church's origin, the secret of the Church's contemporary being, the goal of the Church's final self-realization on behalf of the human race. The Word and the Sacraments in the midst of the Church make known to its members continually what is their origin, their secret and their goal. For the *Word* is the Word of the Cross, whereby the Church is made, renewed and judged. The *Eucharist* is the proclaiming of the Lord's death until his coming again; the setting forth before God and man of the whole drama of his life, death resurrection and parousia; and the feeding of his people with his broken body and outpoured blood."[28]

# Notes

1. From the concluding doxology to the second, third and fourth Eucharistic Prayers in the Rite A Order for Holy Communion in *The Alternative Service Book 1980*.
2. *Birth by Drowning* is the title of a verse play by Norman Nicholson (Faber & Faber, London, 1960), telling the story of Elisha and Naaman the leper. 'As you deduce,' writes Mr Nicholson in a private letter, 'the phrase refers, by implication, to baptism, though this is not specifically the subject of the play.'
3. *The Rites of the Catholic Church: Christian Initiation* (Pueblo Publishing, N.Y., 1976) section 215, pp.96-97.
4. *The Alternative Service Book 1980, Initiation Services.* p.231 or p.246.
5. R.C.D.Jasper and P.F.Bradshaw, *A Companion to the Alternative Service Book* (SPCK, London, 1986) pp.355-356.
6. It should be said that many early baptismal fonts were insufficiently deep for complete immersion; some had running water, some had a spout arrangement at the water inlet so that water could be poured over a candidate's head - see J.G.Davies, *The Architectural Setting of Baptism* (Barrie and Rockliff, 1962) pp.23-26.
7. *The Rites*, op.cit., para.1, p.3, citing Second Vatican Council, Decree on the Church's Missionary Activity, *Ad Gentes*, para.14.
8. *Serm.* cclxxi (*PL* Vol.38). Cited by K.D.MacKenzie, *The Relation of Confirmation to Baptism* in *Confirmation* (SPCK, London, 1926) Vol.1, p.288.
9. *Baptism, Eucharist and Ministry*, World Council of Churches, Faith and Order Paper No.111, (Geneva, 1982) para.14, pp.4-6.
10. *NEH*, 101 (*EH* 125), *Ad cenam Agni providi*, 7th cent.
11. C.K.Barrett, *The Gospel According to S.John* (2nd Edn., SPCK, London, 1978) pp. 554-556.
12. For a summary see R.E.Brown, *The Gospel According to John XIII-XXI* (Anchor Bible, 1966) pp. 944-956.
13. Tertullian, *De Anima*, cap. xliii.
14. John Chrysostom, Homilies on S.John LXXXV, *Library of the Fathers* Vol.36, (Oxford, 1852).
15. O.Cullmann, *Early Christian Worship* (SCM, London, 1978) pp.114-116.
16. The *Asperges* were introduced into the liturgy early in the eighth century and Bede (d.735), commenting on the text *Vidi Aquam*, observed that as the door of Solomon's Temple was on the right, so it was the right side of the Saviour which was to be opened by the spear thrust. *In libros regum, PL* 91:722, and *De templo Salomonis, PL* 91:753-4.
17. BEM. op.cit., *Eucharist* para 1, p.10.
18. ibid. para 14, p.13.
19. The phrase is S.Augustine's: "This is the whole Christ: Christ united with the Church." *In Ps. xc, Sermo* 2.
20. ARCIC, *The Final Report* (CTS, SPCK, London, 1982), Eucharistic Doctrine (1971), para 5, p.14.
21. ibid. para 6, p.14.
22. F.-X.Durrwell C.SS.R., *The Resurrection* (Sheed & Ward, London, 1960) p.347.
23. Flannery, op.cit. cap.III, para 81, p.24.

24.   It should be said that there are two theologies of death at work in the Missal of Paul VI – the first, with an emphasis upon a place with the saints, rest, light and so on, comes from the Gelasian and Gregorian and later sacramentaries; the second, placing the emphasis on the Resurrection and entry into the Pascal Mystery, reflects the exhortation in *Sacrosanctum Concilium* mentioned above. As a matter of practice it is even possible to select whole formularies which have the first theology exclusively and no paschal references.

25.   see G.Rowell, *The Liturgy of Christian Burial* (Alcuin Club Collections No.59, London, 1977), especially Chapter 6.

26.   *LHWE* op.cit. note 5 p.227.

27.   Maria Boulding, *A Touch of God*, (SPCK, London, 1982), p.46.

28.   A.M. Ramsay, *The Resurrection of Christ* (Revised Edn., Fontana, Glasgow, 1961) p.97.

# Chapter V

# The Mystery of the Cross

As Lent moves closer towards Holy week we can hardly avoid being aware of a change of atmosphere. The last fortnight in Lent is no longer called Passiontide in either the Roman or Anglican traditions but a gradually heightening intensity in this second part of Lent does aim at concentrating all our attention on the Cross[1]. This is effected not only by the readings but in particular by the Proper Prefaces. One of those provided in the *Alternative Service Book* highlights the mystery of the Cross in a very traditional but striking way:

> And now we give you thanks because for our salvation he was obedient even to death on the cross. The tree of shame was made the tree of glory; and where life was lost, there life has been restored.[2]

In this preface we are confronted with the vision of a life-giving tree like the tree which God commanded Moses to cast into the waters of Marah to turn their bitterness into sweetness (Exodus 15:22-25); it is the tree of life of which the Apocalypse also speaks – "the leaves of which are the cure for the nations" (Rev 22:2). Ultimately in this preface we are taken back to the Garden of Eden and reminded that in the Cross (and the Cross is already radiant with the light of the Resurrection) we have not only a new Exodus, but a new Creation. John Donne also reminds us of this in his *Hymn to God my God, in my Sickness*:

We think that Paradise and Calvarie,
Christs Crosse and Adams tree, stood in one place;
Looke, Lord, and finde both Adams met in me;
As the first Adams sweat surrounds my face,
May the last Adams blood my soule embrace.

Donne's allusion is to a very ancient tradition which represents an attempt to explain why the place of Christ's crucifixion should have been called Golgotha – in Aramaic
*gulgulta* – the place of the skull. The legend is that the skull
in question was that of Adam, buried there by his third son,
Seth. Pips from the fruit of the Tree of Life were placed
under Adam's tongue at his burial. From these seeds grew
two trees which were cut down to provide wood for the cross
on which Christ was crucified. This cross, in turn, was raised
over Adam's grave, its shaft driven downwards into the
cavern where his bones lay. Thus the blood and water
pouring from the Saviour's side flowed over the head of
Adam and with him the whole of humanity was cleansed.
The story is rounded off in a truly poetic way as the body of
Christ is seen as a precious bloom flowering on the cross, a
new blossom on old wood. This tale was retold in the
thirteenth century by Jacobus de Voragine in *The Golden
Legend* and passed into English literature when that compila-
tion was translated and printed by William Caxton in 1483[3].

The images in the story are tremendously powerful. Christ,
who is our life, triumphs over death. His victory definitively
conquers death; for that which is dead is made eternally alive.
The tree of life which had withered and died, blossoms into
life on the grave of him whose sin was the cause of the
whole process. Here we have what S.Paul so cogently
explained to the Corinthians, "Just as all die in Adam, so in
Christ will all be brought to life." (1 Cor 15:21).

S.Paul's teaching is here one of solidarity – the solidarity
of the whole human race, solidarity in the sin of the first
Adam and its consequences, and again solidarity in the
resurrection of the second Adam – Christ. As the race of
Adam, we share in his fall but because we are baptized into
Christ's death, we are able to share in his life. Whereas the
bones of the first Adam moulder at the foot of the Cross, the

body of the second Adam blossoms into life on the wood of the tree. Adam is baptized by the blood and water from the Saviour's side and redeemed. For Christ's victory over the "old serpent" would not have been complete, had he not delivered Adam from his power. The skull and bones at the bottom of a crucifix or icon serve not only as a reference to locale but also as an indication of purpose.

The beautiful images of this legend find powerful expression in the hymn of Venantius Fortunatus, written in 569 to celebrate the solemn reception at Poitiers of a relic of the True Cross and, as we have already observed, now used in the Liturgy of the Lord's Passion on Good Friday and, in the Latin edition of the Roman Office, as the office hymn at the Office of Readings and Matins throughout Holy Week.

> God in pity saw man fallen,
> Shamed and sunk in misery,
> When he fell on death by tasting
> Fruit of the forbidden tree;
> Then another tree was chosen
> Which the world from death should free.
>
> Thus the scheme of our salvation
> Was of old in order laid,
> That the manifold deceiver's
> Art by art might be outweighed,
> And the lure the foe put forward
> Into means of healing made.
>
> Faithful Cross! above all other,
> One and only noble tree!
> None in foliage, none in blossom,
> None in fruit thy peer may be;
> Sweetest wood and sweetest iron!
> Sweetest weight is hung on thee. [4]

Contemporary with Venantius Fortunatus and expressing visually much the same sense of awe and mystery is the great apse mosaic of the Cross in Sant'Apollinare in Classe, just outside Ravenna. Here the victory of the cross, raised triumphant like a great jewelled throne on a star spangled sky, initiates the transfiguration of the whole cosmos. In its place of honour, dominating the whole basilica, the richly adorned cross has been lifted high into the heavens to become the focal point of a new order. The idea is very much that expressed in the apocryphal 3rd-century Acts of Andrew:

> I know thy mystery for which thou art set up: for thou art planted in the earth, and securely set in the depth, that thou mayest join the things that are in the earth and that are under the earth unto the heavenly things. O Cross, device of the salvation of the Most High! O Cross, trophy of the victory of Christ over the enemies! O Cross, planted upon earth and having thy fruit in the heavens! O name of the Cross, a thing filled with all![5]

We have spoken of the 'Mystery of the Cross' and of the 'Paschal Mystery' and sampled a little of the results of the fascination they have held for early Christian thinkers, poets and artists: at this point perhaps we need to look a little closer at our use of the word 'mystery' since it is a key word in theology and a word we can easily misunderstand.

First of all, we need to note that in Christian language we often use the word 'mysteries' in the plural in speaking of separate events in the history of our redemption, as, for example, in the fifteen mysteries of the Rosary. In the New Testament however the mystery is one and indivisible, whether it is spoken of as "the mystery of God," "the mystery of his purpose," "the mystery of Christ," "the mystery of the Gospel," or simply "the mystery" (cf. Col 2:2; Eph 1:9; 3:4; 6:19; 3:3 and elsewhere). This is not to suggest that it is wrong to use the word in the plural, since, for example, our use of the phrase the "Holy Mysteries" to describe the Eucharist and the general use of the word *mysteria* in Greek to denote what in Latin came to be called *sacramenta* can be traced back to Pauline usage, and particularly perhaps to his reference to the "stewards entrusted with the mysteries of God" (1 Cor 4:1). Nevertheless essentially there is still only one mystery.

Mystery is a word we can use in a purely secular context. In this sense it is something which baffles the mind and which eludes a solution because the essential key to its understanding has been lost, kept secret, or hidden. A mystery in this sense is something which demands a solution and which once solved is no longer a mystery. The word is also used sometimes to describe something which has an atmosphere of the irrational and the occult – the world of magic, ghosts and spirits. Mystery in this sense can never be understood because it completely defies all rational explanation. It is in this latter sense that the word is sometimes used quite wrongly in a Christian context, as for example when those who in a wholesale fashion oppose all liturgical reform and cling obstinately to what Archbishop Cranmer calls "dark and dumb ceremonies,"[6] which are so obscure or archaic that they have lost the power to communicate any meaning, do so in the interests of maintaining an "atmosphere of mystery" or the "mysterious quality" of Christian worship. Christian worship must indeed express the dimension of mystery but this must not be confused with mere mysteriousness.

The best starting point for considering the specifically New Testament idea of mystery is S.Paul's first letter to the Corinthians. There S.Paul contrasts the preaching of the Cross – "to the Jews an obstacle they cannot get over, to the gentiles foolishness" – with the wisdom of the world. He is concerned to show that though it seems to a merely worldly wisdom to be utter foolishness there is a true wisdom of God; indeed it is Christ himself who is "both the power of God and the wisdom of God" (1 Cor 1: 17–31). He then goes on to tell us a little bit more about this wisdom.

To those who have reached maturity, we do talk of a wisdom, not, it is true, a philosophy of this age or of the rulers of this age, who will not last long now. It is of the mysterious wisdom of God that we talk, the wisdom that was hidden, which God predestined to be for our glory before the ages began. None of the rulers of the age recognised it; for if they had recognised it, they would not have crucified the Lord of glory; but it is as scripture says:
What no eye has seen and no ear has heard,
what the mind of man cannot visualize;
all that God has prepared for those who love him,

to us, though, God has given revelation through the Spirit, for the Spirit explores the depths of everything, even the depths of God. (1 Cor 2:6-10)

The key idea here is of an eternal wisdom of God - God's plan of redemption and glorification for his creation - which is inaccessible to man except through the revelation of the Spirit and which has been made known "in a mystery" in the Cross of Christ. We find this key idea in other epistles, as when S.Paul speaks of the "mystery which for endless ages was kept secret but now (as the prophets wrote) is revealed, as the eternal God commanded, to be made known to all the nations." (Romans 16:25-26) and of "the message which was a mystery hidden for generations and for centuries and has now been revealed to his holy people" (Col 1:25-26).

S.Paul borrowed this idea of a "mystery" of wisdom, long hidden in the mind of God but now made manifest, from Jewish apocalyptic (Dan 2:18-19) where it seems to be a concept of Persian origin. The term is also found in the Qumran literature where it is used with some of the profundity with which S.Paul invests it, but he enriches it immeasurably by applying it to salvation's climactic moment: the saving Cross of Christ and its consequence - the restoration of all things in Christ. There have been hints and glimpses and prophecies of this revelation in the Old Testament, but it is only in Christ that this mystery has been brought from eternity into time, has been disclosed and revealed to us. For us Christians therefore the mystery is not something *hidden*; it is the exact opposite, it is something *revealed*. Yet having been revealed it remains a mystery, for it possesses a depth which far exceeds the grasp of human understanding: "now we only see reflections in a mirror" (1 Cor 13:12).

This Mystery of the Gospel is the whole movement of Christ's passage to the Father as the pioneer of our salvation and the first-born among many brethren, a movement that stretches from the Incarnation to the *Parousia* but is concentrated in the Cross and Resurrection. The Paschal Mystery is not so much one part or element in this Mystery of the Gospel as the whole mystery seen in the light of its central and essential dimension. "The centre of Apostolic Christianity," writes Michael Ramsey, "is *Crucifixion- Resurrection*; not Crucifixion alone nor Resurrection alone, nor even Crucifixion as the prelude and Resurrection as the finale but the blending of the two . . . for Life-through-Death is the principle of Jesus's whole life: it is the inward essence of the life of the Christians; and it is the unveiling of the glory of the eternal God."[7]

But the Mystery of Christ is not only revealed to our minds as a Word we must hear and ponder and obey; it is actually communicated to us as a saving reality which breaks in upon our lives. For the Mystery is not something which lies totally outside us; we are included within it, since God, as the author of the Letter to the Ephesians says:

> has let us know the mystery of his purpose, according to his good pleasure which he determined beforehand in Christ, for him to act upon when the times had run their course: that he would bring everything together under Christ, as head, everything in the heavens and everything on earth (Eph 1:9-10).

The Mystery is a mystery of unity, the nuptial mystery of Christ and the Church (Eph 5:32). S.Paul also can say "how rich is the glory of this mystery among the gentiles; it is Christ among you, your hope of glory" (Col 1:27).

The Mystery is of Christ *in us*, because he works out the mystery of his death and resurrection in our lives, leading us along the path which he has pioneered, associating us with himself in his own passage to the Father. The Christian life therefore, cannot adequately be described as "the imitation of Christ": such a one-sided view called forth the classic protest of Dom Denys Prideaux, the first Abbot of Nashdom - "Copy Christ? You *cannot* copy Christ!" "For him," it has been written, "the Christian life could never be the attempt to reach an external conformity with a historical model: it was an internal communion of spirit, in which divine grace operated to remould the personality from within."[8] Imitation can only be imitation from within: it is dependant upon incorporation into Christ, and without this it is both impossible and meaningless.

The Paschal Mystery of Christ's death and resurrection is rooted solidly in unrepeatable historical events and yet it makes contact with us today, it is made present to us here and now, in order to insert us into itself. The Mystery is present and active in the Church and in the Church's sacraments because the dynamic and redeeming power and energy of Christ's death and resurrection are present and active there. Moreover Christ himself is always present in his Church – present in a particular manner in the eucharistic banquet but present also in all the sacraments and in the ministry of the Word; and he is present as the risen and exalted and glorified Lord, who was once slain, and who bears even now in his body the marks of the Passion, but is now alive for evermore, reigning with the Father and the Holy Spirit in the glory of the Trinity. We can go even further and say with Charles Davis, that "while the mystery of salvation was realized historically in the unique events of Christ's life, death and resurrection, its reality on its deepest level transcended history. What was its deepest reality? It was the enduring act of love in Christ. The mystery of salvation is the mystery of the divine *agape*. This came into the world in Christ and found expression in the human love of the incarnate Son of God... it gave redemptive value to all the events of the *transitus*; it was their deepest reality."[9] The sacrifice of the incarnate Christ has behind it the eternal exchange of love within the Trinity, and in particular the movement of filial love and homage rendered by the Son to the Father. Michael Ramsey can speak of "the unveiling of the glory of the eternal God" in the death and resurrection of Christ because those events give us a glimpse into the very heart of the Godhead, the exchange of love within the Blessed Trinity.

In the Liturgy of Good Friday a large wooden crucifix is brought through the church into the sanctuary and there solemnly lifted up for the veneration of the people: "This is the wood of the cross, on which hung the Saviour of the

world. Come let us worship." In one permitted form of this
showing of the Cross it is a veiled cross which is brought
into the church and there gradually unveiled. It is indeed
true that the Cross is an unveiling; it is the revelation of the
mystery hidden and kept secret for long ages and it enables
us to gaze at the deepest and most sacred of all mysteries,
and not only to gaze but to be taken up to share and to
participate in it. "The liturgy is the mystery of Christ made
present to us," writes Charles Davis, "It is a symbolic
representation of the saving work of Christ in which the
reality of that work becomes present. How is it present? It
is present in so far as it is reproduced in us by the present
action of the risen Christ. Our sacramental life is an image
of the life of Christ, and we are conformed to Christ in the
mystery of his *transitus*. But this is also brought about, not
only by the present action of Christ, but also by the active
influence of the acts that made up his redemptive work.
These are present by their dynamic power, so that the total
mystery of Christ in its historical realization acts on us in
the liturgy and is the cause of our own participation in the
mystery. Finally, the inner core of that redemptive work,
since it transcends time, still exists, and hence is made
present as an existing reality by means of the liturgical
representation."[10]

All this leads us up to a view of the liturgy of Holy Week
and Easter which sees it not as a series of dramatic
ceremonies to kindle our imagination and so help us to
reconstruct for our own devotion the passion and resurrection of our Lord but rather as a real presence of the Paschal
Mystery with us here and now. As Adrian Nocent writes,
"The liturgy, after all, is not simply a play. We do not take
part in the liturgy in order to recall past events in an
atmosphere of spiritual emotion. We take part in it in order
to celebrate a mystery that the liturgy itself renders
present"[11]. This surely is the significance of the carving on
the Paschal Candle not only of a cross and the letters Alpha
and Omega but also of the numerals of the current "year of
grace." "Christ yesterday and today," proclaims the celebrant as he traces the inscription, "the beginning and the
end, Alpha and Omega; all time belongs to him and all the

ages; to him be glory and power, through every age and for ever. Amen."

Because the mystery of the Cross (and in this phrase we must include the resurrection as well as the death of Christ) shines forth as the whole Christian gospel in its concentrated essence, we can see that Holy Week and Easter must stand on a different footing from all other feasts of the Christian Year. This is to some extent demonstrated in T.S.Eliot's well-known version of S.Thomas Becket's Christmas sermon: "I wish only that you should meditate in your hearts the deep meaning and mystery of our masses of Christmas Day. For whenever Mass is said, we re-enact the Passion and Death of our Lord; and on this Christmas Day we do this in celebration of his Birth."[12]

Many of the Fathers attributed to the Pascha the character of a mystery or sacrament; S.Leo in his sermons refers several times to the *sacramentum* of the Cross or of the Pascha. We must remember that during his time (he was Pope from 440 to 461) there was no separate commemoration of the Crucifixion on what is now Good Friday, so that when he describes the Cross of Christ as "both *sacramentum* and example"[13] and when he talks of the "*paschale sacramentum*"[14] he is pointing to one reality and one liturgical celebration - *sacramento Dominicae passionis et resurrectionis*"[15]; in the same way, when he says that the gospel narrative which his flock have just heard presents to them the whole paschal mystery - *totum paschale sacramentum* - he is referring to the reading of the narrative of both the Passion and the Resurrection at the Easter Vigil[16].

There is of course, together with an undeniable richness,a real lack of precision in this kind of 'sacramental' language; only in a somewhat difficult and obscure passage from one of S.Augustine's letters do we find an attempt at definition. The Bishop of Hippo makes a sharp distinction between a feast like Christmas, which is only the memorial or commemoration of a past event, and Easter, which can be called a sacrament because in it we not only commemorate the historical event of Christ's death and resurrection but also celebrate our own passage from death to life; he argues that this should be evident from the very word Pascha which is properly translated *transitus* – passage from death to life.[17]

In the 20th century it has become possible to speak once again of "the Sacrament of Easter." On the eve of the Second Vatican Council the French liturgical scholar, Antoine Chavasse, could write; "In celebrating the death and resurrection of Christ the Church does not simply recall a past historical event. She celebrates 'sacramentally' the mystery of salvation and in evoking the death and resurrection of Christ she actualizes their mysterious power of influence. The mystery of Easter is thus at the same time the mystery of Christ, the Head , and the mystery of the Church, the Body of Christ. In the Paschal Vigil Christ applies to his Church in a more special way the saving power of his death and resurrection, and the means of his intervention is this very celebration which the Church is making."[18]

After the Council this approach was to be more authoritatively and more publicly set forth by Paul VI in the *motu proprio* by which he gave approval to the reform of the liturgical year and in which he referred back to the teaching of some of his more immediate predecessors:

These popes, together with the Fathers and the tradition of the Catholic Church, taught that the historical events by which Christ Jesus won our salvation through his death are not merely commemorated or recalled in the course of the liturgical year, even though they instruct and nourish the least educated among the faithful. These pontiffs taught rather that the celebration of the liturgical year exerts 'a special sacramental power and influence which strengthens Christian life.' We ourselves believe and profess this same truth.[19]

Each year therefore as Holy Week and Easter come round once more we should approach them as we would approach a sacrament, a grace-bearing sign which is able to effect what it signifies. The Sacrament of Easter demands from us a total commitment: we are called upon to live the liturgy of these days in such a way as to lay ourselves open to be assimilated to the mystery it celebrates. We must so enter into the passage of Christ to the Father that we celebrate at the same time our own passage to the Father. We have to enter deeply into the fellowship of Christ's sufferings so that we may know fully and joyfully the power of his resurrection.

## Notes

1.  According to the former Roman rite all images, including crucifixes, were to be covered with purple veiling during Passiontide; the older usage was to veil them from the beginning of Lent and mediaeval English usage prescribed unbleached linen for this purpose. The 1969 Commentary of the Sacred Congregation of Rites on the Revised Liturgical Year and New Roman Calendar explained the suppression of Passiontide ("to preserve the unity of Lent") and ruled that the veiling of crosses and images was no longer required except where the local episcopal conference decided that the practice was still useful.
2.  *ASB*, Rite A Order for Holy Communion, Preface 10, p.155. This same preface was provided in the former Roman Missal for Passiontide and Feasts of the Holy Cross and is to be found in the new Missal as the Preface o. the Triumph of the Cross (P46). Its origin is uncertain but goes back at least to the ninth century; the theme of the two trees however, can be traced back to a passage from S.Irenaeus at the end of the second century (*Adversus Haereses* V, 17,3), which can be found as the second reading in the Office of Readings for Friday in the second week of Advent.
3.  W.Caxton (trans.), *The Golden Legend* (7 Vols. J.M.Dent, London, 1900) Vol 3, pp.169 ff.
4.  *EH*, 95 & 96. The version in *NEH* (517) omits the second of the three verses we have quoted.
5.  M.R.James (Trans.) *The Apocryphal New Testament* (Oxford, 1924 – reprinted 1975) p.359-360.
6.  *Book of Common Prayer*: Preface - *Of Ceremonies*.
7.  A.M.Ramsey, op.cit. pp.20-21. (*The Resurrection of Christ*)
8.  *The Jubilee Book of the Benedictines of Nashdom, 1914-1964* (Faith Press, London, 1964) p.49.
9.  C.Davis, *Liturgy and Doctrine* (Sheed & Ward, London, 1960) pp.71-72.
10. ibid. pp.73-74.
11. Adrian Nocent O.S.B., Trans. M.J.O'Connell, *The Liturgical Year* (4 Vols, Collegeville, Minnesota, 1977) Vol 2 - Lent and Holy Week - p.187.
12. T.S.Eliot, *Murder in the Cathedral* (Faber & Faber, London, 1935), p.47 (3rd Edn.)
13. Sermon 72.
14. Sermon 47.
15. Sermon 51.

16. Sermon 72.
17. *Epistola 55* (*Ad Inquisitiones Januarii*); see L.Bouyer, *Life & Liturgy*, p.205
18. A.Chavasse, "*Le Cycle Pascal*" in *L'Eglise en Prière: Introduction à la Liturgie* ed. A.G.Martimort (Desclée & Cie, Tournai, 1961), p.695.
19. Apostolic Letter of 14th Feb 1969, *Mysterii Paschalis*, reproduced in the introductory material of the new Roman Missal and quoting *Maxima Redemptionis Nostrae Mysteria*, the decree of the S.C.R. setting out the liturgical reform cf Holy Week under Pius XII in 1955. In contrast with the teaching of S.Augustine these two papal texts attach a sacramental quality to the liturgical year as a whole. So in her book, *The Coming of God*, (SPCK, London, 1982) Maria Boulding can entitle one of her chapters *The Sacrament of Advent.*
20. John Donne *"Hymn to God my God, in my Sickness"*

# Chapter VI

# The Great and Holy Week

Although in the wider movement of liturgical renewal
Roman Catholics and Anglicans have often been moving at
the same pace as well as in the same direction, in the
narrower context of the reform of liturgical texts, a striking
contrast presents itself. This reform can really be said to
have started in the Roman Catholic Church with the
restoration of the Easter Vigil. It is sometimes too easily
assumed by those who have insufficient acquaintance with
the facts that the present reform of the texts of the Roman
liturgy began with, or immediately after, the Second
Vatican Council. In fact it really began in 1951 when Pope
Pius XII promulgated a revised Easter Vigil for use at night,
as an optional alternative to the Vigil ceremonies and First
Mass of Easter celebrated, according to the rubrics then in
force, on Holy Saturday morning. This was followed up in
1955 when new liturgical texts for the rest of Holy Week
were introduced and the revised Easter Vigil became
obligatory. Although further changes were made at the time
of the promulgation of the new Roman Missal under Paul
VI in 1969, the main features of the reform undertaken
under Pius XII have been respected and continued. In the
Church of England on the other hand – although this is not
true of other churches of the Anglican Communion – the
present process of the reform of liturgical texts can almost
be said to have ended with the publication in 1986 of a
volume of services and prayers for *Lent, Holy Week, Easter*,
commended by the House of Bishops. One of the most
obvious weaknesses of the 1980 *Alternative Service Book*

was its failure to provide in any clear or coherent way for the liturgy of Holy Week; such provision as was made is not only supplemented, but to a considerable extent corrected, by *Lent, Holy Week, Easter.* The latter however does not have the same degree of canonical authority as the *Alternative Service Book* and, unlike the Roman Order, it is more in the nature of "a *directory* from which choices may be made;" it is "a manual to be used with selectivity, sensitivity and imagination."[1]

Liturgical scholars may be able to draw more general conclusions from this curious contrast, but there are certain obvious reasons for it. The Easter Vigil, the Palm Sunday procession, the Altar of Repose on Maundy Thursday and the Veneration of the Cross on Good Friday were all suppressed in the Church of England during the sixteenth century and found no place in any of the successive editions of the Book of Common Prayer. Their revival, or partial revival, towards the end of the nineteenth century by the Ritualists was regarded as both flagrantly illegal and horribly superstitious by their opponents, and it is only comparatively recently that moderate and evangelical Anglicans have come to look with a more favourable eye at the rites of Holy Week as they have become increasingly sacramentally and liturgically conscious[2].

Roman Catholics had a quite different problem; they had a Holy Week liturgy but it was not feeding and inspiring the thinking or the praying of either the laity (who preferred other forms of devotion) or the clergy (who tended to regard the Holy Week rites simply as a necessary duty to be accomplished out of obedience). The problem was not only one of language (Latin) but also one of timing. The Maundy Thursday mass was celebrated early on Thursday morning, the Good Friday Mass of the Presanctified was also usually celebrated early in the morning, while an Easter Vigil solemnly celebrated on Holy Saturday morning, with the Deacon singing eloquently – albeit in Latin – of the glories of this *vere beata nox*, was not a natural focus of devotion for the faithful. So the Liturgical Movement, begun (so far as such a thing can be dated) in Belgium before the First

World War under the leadership of Dom Lambert Beauduin, was bound sooner rather than later to feel particularly
frustrated by the Babylonish Captivity of the Easter Vigil.
The pressure for change came both from the world of
liturgical and historical scholarship, particularly that of
Dom Odo Casel of Maria Laach, who published in Germany
an important study of Easter in the Patristic Church in
1938[3], and from that of pastoral liturgy, and it is not
without significance that in 1945, in its first year of
publication, the influential French review *La Maison-Dieu*
contained a plea for the restoration of the Vigil. So the
reforms of 1951 and 1955 not only put an end to the
anomaly of a nocturnal celebration performed in full
daylight; they also changed the times of the Maundy
Thursday and Good Friday celebrations, shortened and
simplified the rites, made full provision for the active
participation of the laity (including the use of the vernacu-
lar for the renewal of baptismal vows at the Vigil) and
introduced a number of changes that were later to be more
generally applied. In 1955 it also became permissible to
choose the ferial Lenten mass in preference to a saint's
feast, a move which went some way to restoring the
integrity of the Great Forty Days. If it is true, as a great
liturgical historian of Holy Week has written, that Easter is
the heart of the liturgy - *Pascha est cor liturgiae*[4] - then the
reform of the liturgical books of the Roman rite began at
the right place.

## THE BEGINNINGS OF HOLY WEEK

In Chapter I we saw that at the time of the First Council of
Nicaea the Pascha was a single, unitive celebration of the
Death, Resurrection and Glorification of Christ, held
during the night of Easter, and we referred to the
introduction later in the fourth century at Jerusalem of an
historical sequence celebrating in chronological order the
separate moments of the Passion story[5]. Now, as we turn to
describe Holy Week as it is celebrated today, it seems
appropriate to discuss this change in more detail. It has to
be said, however, that the particularly rich deposit of

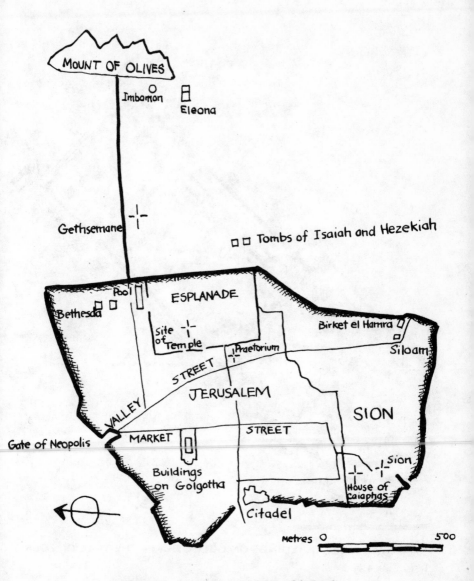

FOURTH-CENTURY JERUSALEM

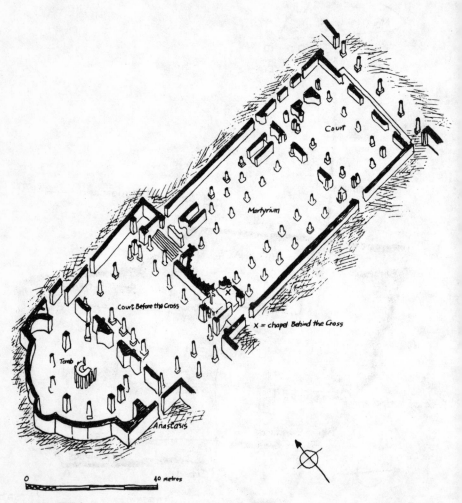

CONSTANTINE'S BUILDINGS ON GOLGOTHA IN THE TIME OF EGERIA

contemporary or near-contemporary documents – eye-witness descriptions, catechetical material and lectionary evidence – from fourth-century Jerusalem has led some scholars, notably Dom Gregory Dix[6], to over-emphasize a Jerusalem-inspired change from an early unitive, eschatological celebration of Easter to a new historical, rememorative Paschal liturgy throughout Christendom. As Talley has pointed out, a sense of liturgical progression through the events of Holy Week can be found in the worship of the Syrian Church in the first half of the third century[7], and as Jungmann has demonstrated, the Roman liturgy always kept its eyes on the whole mystery of the Passion and never completely abandoned a unitive approach[8]. Nevertheless, it is impossible to understand Holy Week as the Church celebrates it in the twentieth century without some understanding of the fourth-century Jerusalem background.

In 1884 a manuscript, lost for seven hundred years, was discovered in Italy; it is part of a travel diary known to liturgical scholars as *Peregrinatio Aetheriae* or now more usually Egeria's *Travels*[9], written by a nun who was probably called Egeria and who seems to have come from the Atlantic coast of Gaul or Spain. Writing for her sisters, she compiled this account of her pilgrimage to the Holy Land and the Near East in the penultimate decade of the fourth century, during the time that S.Cyril was Bishop of Jerusalem. Of particular importance to us is her very detailed description of the events of 'the Great Week' as kept in Jerusalem. It is clear that she describes these events in such detail for her sisters because they would have been totally unfamiliar to them; this becomes obvious when she comes to the Easter Vigil which she does *not* describe, recording simply that "they keep their paschal vigil like us" and only describing one addition, a detail peculiar to Jerusalem[10].

The origin of our Palm Sunday can be found in her description of a ceremony held in the early evening:

At 5 o'clock the passage is read from the Gospel about the children who met the Lord with palm branches, saying, 'Blessed is he that cometh in the name of the

Lord.' At this the bishop and all the people rise from
their places, and start off on foot down from the
summit of the Mount of Olives. All the people go before
him with psalms and antiphons, all the time repeating,
'Blessed is he that cometh in the name of the Lord.'
The babies and the ones too young to walk are carried
on their parents' shoulders. Every one is carrying
branches, either palm or olive, and they accompany the
bishop in the very way the people did when once they
went down with the Lord. They go on foot all down the
Mount to the city, and all through the city to the
Anastasis[11], but they have to go pretty gently on
account of the older women and men among them who
might get tired.

As far as Maundy Thursday is concerned, Egeria describes
two celebrations of the Eucharist in the late afternoon or
early evening. The second seems to have been the more
solemn of the two and it takes place at the spot she calls
*Behind the Cross*, a chapel enclosing a stump of rock that
was believed to be Golgotha. She notes that this is the only
day of the year that the Eucharist is celebrated in that place
"and everyone receives Communion." After this Eucharist
"everybody hurries home for a meal" and then begins a
continuous round of prayer and vigil, stations being held
with appropriate readings and prayers at the Mount of
Olives and in the Garden of Gethsemane and in the city for
the narrative of Christ's trial before Pilate. Some then go
home for a short rest "before the sun is up"; the more
courageous go to pray at the Column of the Flagellation.

This brings us without any real break to Good Friday.
The faithful are summoned to be present at Golgotha at 8
o'clock in the morning and the bishop's chair is placed
there:

A table is placed before him with a cloth on it, the
deacons stand round, and there is brought to him a gold
and silver box containing the holy Wood of the Cross.
It is opened, and the Wood of the Cross and the Title
are taken out and placed on the table. As long as the
holy Wood is on the table, the bishop sits with his

hands resting on either end of it and holds it down, and the deacons round him keep watch over it. They guard it like this because what happens now is that all the people, catechumens as well as faithful, come up one by one to the table. They stoop down over it, kiss the Wood, and move on. But one one occasion (I don't know when) one of them bit off a piece of the holy Wood and stole it away, and for this reason the deacons stand around and keep watch in case anyone dares to do the same again.

This obviously takes a long time, from 8 o'clock to midday. At midday a Three Hours' Liturgy of the Word is held in the open courtyard between the Chapel of the Cross and the Anastasis. It concludes at 3 o'clock with "the reading from S.John's Gospel about Jesus giving up the ghost." There is then a further service in the Great Church at the end of which all go to the Anastasis:

> where, once inside, they read the Gospel passage about Joseph asking Pilate for the Lord's body and placing it in a new tomb. After the reading there is a prayer, the blessing of the catechumens and faithful, and the dismissal.

Egeria's account helps us to understand how our present Holy Week and so many of its ceremonies could only have originated in Jerusalem, almost certainly as a result of the keen pastoral and pedagogical sensitivity and imagination of a great teaching bishop, S.Cyril of Jerusalem, whose catechetical and mystagogical discourses we have referred to already in connection with Lent[12]. Moreover they could only have developed after the Constantinian Peace of the Church, which led to the excavation of the Holy Places, with which the name of the Emperor's mother, S.Helena, is traditionally associated. The rediscovery of the Holy Places resulted in their being opened up for the devotion of the faithful, not just the Christian community in Jerusalem, but also the new wave of pilgrims which these developments encouraged. The new accessibility of the actual sites where the separate events of the Passion had taken place could not have failed to affect liturgical performance. The impression made on the pilgrims – notably on Egeria herself – by Holy Week and Easter spent in Jerusalem helps us to understand how the special ceremonies of the Jerusalem liturgy came eventually to be exported to other parts of the Christian world.

One factor contributing to this evolution was the dissemination of relics of the True Cross to other Christian centres, which was held to justify the adoption in such places of the Jerusalem rite of veneration. The pre-eminent example of this is the Roman basilica called *Santa Croce in Gerusalemme* (Holy Cross in Jerusalem). The earliest account of this church, actually called Jerusalem, comes from a fourth-century biography of Sylvester I, the pope who had the satisfaction of seeing Rome transformed from a pagan into a Christian city through the generosity of the Emperor Constantine. We read that, "Constantine opened a basilica in the Sessorian Palace, where, in a golden reliquary, are kept pieces of the Holy Cross, and named it Jerusalem." Little of the Constantinian basilica remains today save eight great granite columns in the otherwise baroque nave, but the subterranean Chapel of S.Helena beneath the modern Relic Chapel was originally a part of the Sessorian Palace. Here the pavement rests on earth brought by S.Helena from Jerusalem, the debris from her excavations on the site of Golgotha and the tomb of Christ. Although it took until some time at the end of the seventh or the beginning of the eighth century for the rite of the Veneration of the Cross at this basilica to establish itself as part of the Papal liturgy (thanks to the influence of a succession of oriental popes), it was a comparatively small step which then led from the veneration of a relic of the True Cross to the veneration of a simple cross and to the consequent spread of the practice to churches which did not possess a relic. In a similar way it was a comparatively small step to free the Palm Sunday procession from its exclusive connection with its original geographical context.

By the end of the fourth century in much of Christendom the separate events of Christ's redemptive *transitus* were celebrated as distinct festivals. The influence of the Jerusalem liturgy and the ceremonies associated with it had helped to create a serial, historical commemoration of these events in Holy Week. By deliberately reconstructing the final events in Jesus's life in a week of celebration the worshipper was led not merely to recall those actions, but also, in some mysterious way, to share in them because, as Leo the Great had already observed, "all that was visible of the Redeemer has passed over into the sacraments"[13]. Hence the tremendous appeal of the Holy Week ceremonies and the desire today to revive them or reclaim them for the whole Church, Eastern and Western, Catholic and Reformed[14].

## THE EASTERN TRADITION

If it is easy to trace the evolution of the Western Holy Week liturgy from the Jerusalem Holy Week described by Egeria, it is less easy to trace it precisely where we might expect to find the evidence to be clearer, in the rites of the Eastern Churches. In a book of limited scope, we cannot begin to do justice to the liturgical complexity and theological richness of the Holy Week and Easter liturgies of the Eastern Orthodox and Oriental Orthodox Churches, but it does seem appropriate to say something briefly at this stage about the present Holy Week and Easter services of the Byzantine Rite.

The Saturday before Holy Week is called the Saturday of the Holy and Righteous Lazarus[15] and one of the *troparia* sung on this day and on Palm Sunday links together these two mysteries in a joyful anticipation of the Resurrection and the Parousia.

> Giving us before thy Passion an assurance of the general resurrection, thou hast raised Lazarus from the dead, O Christ our God. Therefore, like the children, we also carry tokens of victory, and cry to thee, the Conqueror of death, Hosanna in the highest; blessed is he that comes in the name of the Lord.

Palm Sunday itself has a blessing of palms but this takes place at Matins.[16] We shall find that many of the most striking (and well-attended) ceremonies are in fact associated

with the Offices rather than the eucharistic liturgy. Thus on
the Monday, Tuesday and Wednesday, although the Liturgy
of the Presanctified is celebrated, the main emphasis is on
(anticipated) Matins. In the Eastern Orthodox Church the
sacrament of the anointing of the sick is usually celebrated on
the evening of Wednesday in Holy Week. As Bishop
Kallistos Ware has remarked:

> All are anointed, whether physically ill or not; for there
> is no sharp line of demarcation between bodily and
> spiritual sicknesses and this sacrament confers not only
> bodily healing but forgiveness of sins, thus serving as a
> preparation for the reception of Holy Communion on the
> next day.[17]

Thursday sees the Eucharist (according to the Liturgy of
S.Basil) celebrated after Vespers, though this now happens in
the morning. In some cathedrals this will be followed by the
Washing of the Feet if the Bishop is celebrating. During the
liturgy in patriarchal churches the Chrism is consecrated. On
Thursday evening there is celebrated Matins of Holy and
Great Friday, a long service that lasts for about five hours; it
is called *The Office of the Holy and Redeeming Passion of
our Lord Jesus Christ* and is centred upon the reading of the
'Twelve Gospels', a narrative of the Passion derived from all
four Gospels and interspersed with troparia, one of which is
almost identical with the Reproaches sung during the Western
Veneration of the Cross on Good Friday.

Good Friday is a strictly aliturgical day; there is no celebra-
tion of the Eucharist, not even the Liturgy of the
Presanctified. The Orthodox Liturgy is familiar with the rite
of the veneration of the Cross; this takes place on the third
Sunday of Lent and on the Feast of the Exaltation of the
Holy Cross on September 14th but not on Good Friday.
Today, at Vespers, the Cross is replaced by the *epitaphion*, a
cloth embroidered with a representation of the deposition of
Christ, which is carried from the altar to a bier decorated with
flowers in the middle of the church, there to receive the
veneration of the faithful. Compline follows immediately
upon Vespers: its popular title is *The Lamentation of the Most*

*Holy Mother of God* and highlights a striking contrast with the Western tradition, which finds no place for the sorrows or the joys of our Lady in strictly liturgical material for Holy Week and Easter, unless one includes one of the Good Friday *Tenebrae* responsories (*Caligeraverunt oculi mei*) and the recitation of the *Regina Coeli* after Compline in Eastertide.

Matins of Holy Saturday, celebrated on Friday evening, sees another procession with the *epitaphion*, carried this time around the outside of the church exactly as at a funeral. The *Trisagion* (Holy God, holy and strong, holy and immortal, have mercy upon us) is sung at this point "to a slow and solemn melody, as at the burial service". Earlier in the service this same note of Easter assurance comes through even more clearly in one of the *troparia*;

> Going down to earth, O Life immortal, thou hast slain hell with the dazzling light of thy divinity. And when thou hadst raised up the dead from their dwelling place beneath the earth, all the powers of heaven cried aloud: Giver of life, O Christ our God, glory to thee.

On the morning of Holy Saturday are celebrated Vespers and the Liturgy (of S.Basil). This rite is in fact the present day descendant of the Easter Vigil, although now celebrated on Saturday morning as a result of the same kind of pressures that caused the Vigil to be celebrated at this time in the West until the reforms of Pius XII. There is a series of fifteen prophetic readings from the Old Testament including the Exodus account of the crossing of the Red Sea. The baptismal reference of the rite is made clear from the beginning of the eucharistic liturgy with the chant "As many of you as were baptized into Christ have put on Christ, alleluia" but at least in the currently received practice of the Russian Church, which dissociates baptisms, weddings and funerals from the celebration of the eucharist, no baptisms now take place at this service. Commenting on this Saturday liturgy Elizabeth Briere writes:

> There is no liturgical moment of the resurrection.

Just as the authentic icon of the resurrection represents Christ, not leaping from the tomb, but trampling on death and hell, so the moment of his rising remains for ever mysterious; we know only that he was dead and is risen, raising up mankind with himself.[18]

The great Easter liturgy itself, celebrated at midnight between Saturday and Sunday, consists of Easter Matins and the Easter Eucharist (according to the Liturgy of S.John Chrysostom). Although it is not, as we have seen, the Easter Vigil, it has become *the* Easter Liturgy, the one and only eucharistic liturgy of Easter Day, and it is a popular and crowded celebration marked with a degree of real joy and genuine and overflowing exuberance which makes our Western celebrations, however much more 'correct', seem pale and lifeless in comparison.

It is the day of Resurrection, O people; let us be enlightened. It is the Passover, the Lord's Passover. For from death to life and from earth to heaven Christ our God has brought us over, singing the hymn of victory.

However different the Easter and Western liturgical traditions now appear, in both the Church of God is celebrating in this great and Holy Week the whole of the Paschal Mystery, refusing to allow its unity to be broken up, even if each day is given over to one particular aspect of it. The unitive and the eschatological are not swallowed up in the rememorative but we continue "to proclaim the Lord's death until he comes" (1 Corinthians 11:26), and acclaim in the Eucharistic Prayer a past event, a present reality and a future expectation:

> Christ *has* died.
> Christ *is* risen.
> Christ *will* come again.

The re-assertion of the unitive character of the Paschal celebration was a a priority in the reform of the Roman Calendar in 1969. As J.D.Crichton has written,

The paschal celebration of the Lord's passion and resurrection at Eastertime is the culminating point of the whole Liturgical Year, it has absolute precedence over all other feasts and celebrations, it is put first in the list of precedence and, to re-establish that it is a unitary celebration of the one Passover, it has been renamed. It is not merely the *Sacrum Triduum* (lit. 'sacred three days') but the *Paschal Triduum* and 'begins with the Evening Mass of the Lord's Supper (on Maundy Thursday), is centred upon the Paschal Vigil and ends with vespers on Easter Day'. Thus is restored to us in its full significance the most ancient celebration of the Christian church. The impression has finally been removed that we were merely celebrating three holy days that 'commemorated' the last events of Christ's life. The three days form a whole in which the church celebrates the whole paschal mystery which is reflected (and participated in) in different ways throughout the period.[19]

## PALM SUNDAY: THE PASSION OF THE LORD

The Roman calendar reforms of 1969 abolished Passion Sunday, which since the seventh century had been the name for the fifth Sunday of Lent, and transferred the name back to Palm Sunday. As in the Gelasian Sacramentary, this now has the Latin title, *Dominica in Palmis, De Passione Domini* which is virtually untranslatable into English. Nevertheless, the restoration of the words 'Of the Lord's Passion' to the ancient title Palm Sunday is significant. The great Passion sermons of S.Leo the Great (pope from 440-461), in which he speaks of the 'indescribable glory of the Passion' as Christ's victory, were preached on this day[20]. The liturgical combination of the joyful entry into Jerusalem and the proclamation of the Passion underlines the Easter significance of all that follows in Holy Week. Palm Sunday celebrates Christ's triumphal entrance into the Holy City to accomplish the Paschal Mystery; in going thus to his death he begins his *transitus*, his return in glory to the Father. The traditional veiling of images and crucifixes has in effect been abolished in the Roman Catholic Church along with Passiontide, though it is still permitted where Bishops' Conferences allow[21]; nevertheless there is an immediate visual difference in today's liturgy since the colour of the vestments used changes from the violet of Lent to the red which will also be used on Good Friday. Passion red expresses neither the unrestrained joy of white nor the dominant penitence of violet but a delicate blend of joy and sorrow, of triumph attained through suffering.

Today's distinctive ceremony, the Commemoration of the Lord's Entry into Jerusalem, should take place before the principal Eucharist and consists of the blessing of palms and a procession together. It is an abuse to separate these two parts either by multiplying the blessing of palms before other celebrations or by omitting the procession altogether, for the palms are blessed entirely in order that they may be carried in the procession. To many people the essence of Palm Sunday has been found in going to church to get a palm cross, but to encourage this attitude by distributing them at services other than the main one or separately from the procession is to deflect attention from the real significance of the ceremony and to risk debasing it to the level of the trivial, the sentimental or even the superstitious. In any case, whatever the devotional appeal today of the dry, woven, palm cross, in procession they have hardly the same symbolic significance as the real green branches of box, yew or willow used in England before the Reformation. In some parts of the country willow branches, with their spring covering of catkins, are still known as 'Palm'. Sprigs from these branches can still be taken away after the service and used to decorate crucifixes or pictures in the home. Whereas in the old rite palms were first blessed and then distributed, in the new rite it is assumed that the people are carrying palm *branches* from the outset which they hold up to be blessed. The implication in the new Roman order that the people have brought the branches to church with them is made explicit in the introduction to the Palm Sunday liturgy in *Lent, Holy Week, Easter*[22].

So much for palms; the procession, with or without them, is far more important as it is the first of the commemorative liturgical actions in Holy Week whereby we involve ourselves in the redemptive movement of Christ's return to the Father. It is highly desirable that the congregation should assemble for the beginning of the service at some suitable place distinct from the church so that the procession can move from one to the other and be clearly seen to effect a solemn entry into the church, just as Christ made his triumphant entry into Jerusalem. Whilst such a procession embodies an element of the dramatic, as do so many of the Jerusalem liturgical ceremonies, it is not just a piece of play-acting or make-believe to stimulate our imagination or heighten our devotion. The Holy Week ceremonies are not designed to *impress* us but rather to *involve* us. This sort of procession is a real act of witness – involving the whole congregation, not just clergy, choir and servers – whereby we pledge our loyalty to Christ, enrol ourselves among his followers and publicly commit ourselves to follow him along the *Via Dolorosa* of his sufferings to the triumph of his resurrection. This is made abundantly clear in the brief introduction supplied in the Roman order for the celebrant to use as he invites the people to take a full part in the celebration:

> Dear friends in Christ, for five weeks of Lent we have been preparing, by works of charity and self-sacrifice, for the celebration of our Lord's paschal mystery. Today we come together to begin this solemn celebration in union with the whole Church throughout the world. Christ entered in triumph into his own city to complete his work as our Messiah: to suffer, to die, and to rise again. Let us remember with devotion this entry which began his saving work and follow him with a lively faith. United with him in his suffering on the cross, may we share his resurrection and new life.[23]

As soon as this explanatory introduction has been read, the people hold up their branches and fronds to be blessed. The prayer in *Lent, Holy Week, Easter* sees the palms as signs of Christ's victory and both Roman and Anglican prayers stress the eschatological theme which is so noticeable in the new rites. The emphasis in the Roman blessing has shifted dramatically from that found in the pre-1955 string of blessing prayers which virtually consecrated the palms, to that in the present choice of two prayers both of which really focus on the people who are about to set forth in procession rather than on the palms they are to carry.

The scene is now set by the reading of the Palm Gospel, which may be taken from any of the Synoptic accounts: Matthew 21:1-11; Mark 11:1-10; or Luke 19:28-40 (the Roman rite permits John 12:12-16 as an alternative in Year B). The celebrant or deacon then bids the procession go forth and so it moves to the church where the eucharist is to be celebrated. The procession is a procession of praise to Jesus the Messiah and so antiphons, psalms and hymns of praise are to be sung as it moves along. It is Christ the King who is acclaimed in these chants, the words of which do not restrict themselves to the Lord's entry into Jerusalem before his passion. Our praises speak also of the resurrection and ascension of Christ, his entry into the *heavenly* Jerusalem, and in so doing we look forward to the final fulfilment of the paschal mystery in the *Parousia*. This is the sense of the Old Testament background: "This is what Yahweh has proclaimed to the remotest part of the earth: Say to the daughter of Zion, 'Look your salvation is coming; with him comes his reward, his achievement precedes him.' " (Isaiah 62:11); "Rejoice heart and soul, daughter of Zion! Shout for joy, daughter of Jerusalem! Look, your king is approaching, he is vindicated and victorious, humble and riding on a donkey, on a colt, the foal of a donkey." (Zechariah 9:9 - this passage is part of that appointed as the first lesson at Morning Prayer in the alternative lectionary provided in *LHWE*); "And suddenly the Lord whom you seek will come to his Temple." (Malachi 3:1). This too is the reason why the Palm Sunday narrative was appointed in the Book of Common Prayer as the Gospel for Advent Sunday; it is a foretaste of the final entry of Christ with the whole company of the redeemed into the fullness of his kingdom. "Lift up your heads O you gates and be lifted up you everlasting doors: and the King of glory shall come in." (Psalm 24: 7).

All this would seem to show that the Commemoration of the Lord's Entry into Jerusalem is not just the historically and sequentially correct way in which to begin the liturgical observance of Holy Week, but it is also theologically the richest and most appropriate. Accordingly, it was regarded as of such importance by the compilers of the 1969 Roman rite that they direct that it must preface every public mass on Palm Sunday. To cope with all circumstances they provide three forms: the Procession, or normative commemoration, described above and followed closely by *LHWE*; the Solemn Entrance, which is to be performed within the church only when circumstances do not permit an extended procession; and a Simple Entrance, in which the commemoration is made with an antiphon and psalm. The Roman rubrics continue hopefully, "Where neither the procession nor the solemn entrance can be celebrated, there should be a bible service on the theme of the Lord's messianic entrance and passion, either on Saturday evening or on Sunday at a convenient time."

There is no longer any discontinuity between the procession and the eucharist, no change from red to violet vestments as there was in the first stage of the reform under Pius XII. The Mass begins almost abruptly; the celebrant, having as it were merely made a more solemn entrance than usual, venerates the altar, omits the penitential rite and begins the Mass with the Collect, much as would have happened in the early days of the Church.

The liturgical emphasis is now firmly on the Passion, but even here we cannot pretend that we are kept in ignorance of the Resurrection. The Collect, essentially the same in Roman and Anglican traditions, sets before us the model of Christ's humility expressed in his suffering, and asks that through following his example we may be made worthy to participate in his resurrection. The first two readings – Isaiah 50: 4–7(9a) and Philippians 2:6(5)–11 – prepare us by providing an interpretative context for the solemn reading of the Passion, taken from a different Synoptic account in each year of a three year cycle. In the reading from Isaiah, taken from the third of the Servant Songs, we cannot help but see a poetic description of the Lord's humiliation and suffering in obedience to his Father's will culminating in his ultimate vindication; the 'Kenotic Hymn' from Philippians 2 makes this even more explicit – God has highly

exalted the Man who humbled himself in obedience even to
the point of giving his life on the Cross and given him the
name that is above every other name.

The reformed liturgy of Palm Sunday perfectly expresses
the essential balance between rememorative and unitive
celebration of the Paschal Mystery. It avoids focussing on
details and incidents which might present a one-sided view
of the Passion in terms solely of suffering and offers instead
the very different insight expressed in the earliest apostolic
sermon, "you can be certain that the Lord and Christ whom
God has made is this Jesus whom you crucified" (Acts
2:36b). The Passion – "Jesus whom you crucified" – can
only be understood in the light of Resurrection-Exalta-
tion – "The Lord and Christ whom God has made" – and so
its liturgical celebration must, in the words of Adrian
Nocent, "give a complete and rounded theological vision of
the mystery of Christ. It tells that this mystery is not a
mystery of death alone but a mystery of life that triumphs
over death. This vision is important for a proper conception
of the spiritual life."[24]

## FROM PALM SUNDAY TO
## MAUNDY THURSDAY

Palm Sunday inaugurates the Great and Holy Week, but
the first three ferial days of the Week, Monday, Tuesday
and Wednesday are distinguished neither by special ceremonies nor today by any attempt to link them chronologi-
cally with particular events in the story of the Passion of
Christ. At one time, however, the names 'Fig' Monday and
'Spy' Wednesday represented a non-liturgical attempt to
link Monday with the cursing of the barren fig tree
(Matthew 21:18-22) and Wednesday with the perfidy of
Judas (Matthew 26:14-16). In the former Roman Missal
the Wednesday retained certain primitive features, notably
two Old Testament lections, a vestige of the time when a
'stational mass' would have been celebrated on this day but
not on Monday or Tuesday. In the middle of the 5th
century, Pope Leo the Great's Passion sermons, begun, as
we have noted above, on the Sunday, were concluded at this

Wednesday stational mass. Today however each of these three days is given two readings only in the Roman Missal, the first being from the Old Testament; *LHWE* gives the same readings and responsorial psalms but provides optional readings from the New Testament epistles and alternative Gospel readings. Both the *Alternative Service Book* and *LHWE* however, following the Book of Common Prayer, assume the use of the Palm Sunday collect on these three days, but the 1979 American Prayer Book does provide a collect for each of these days, one of which will be familiar to many English Anglicans through Eric Milner-White's *A Procession of Passion Prayers*[25]. It is perhaps worth mentioning at this point that it is hardly appropriate on Maundy Thursday to use at Morning Prayer in the Anglican rite the collect provided for the evening eucharist; either the Palm Sunday collect or the second of the two *ASB* collects should be used.

The *day* of the Thursday in Holy Week is the last day of Lent; the Paschal Triduum does not begin until the evening, but that fact explains the absence of any eucharistic celebration on the morning of that Thursday. The only exception allowed is the Mass of the Chrism, normally celebrated by the Diocesan Bishop in his Cathedral on this morning but often – for pastoral reasons – anticipated on one of the earlier days of Holy Week. However, the so-called Gelasian Sacramentary, which may in part represent usage in Rome before the year 700, provides three mass formulae for Thursday. The second and third of these represent the masses with which we are familiar today, the Chrism Mass (*Missa Chrismatis*) and the Evening Mass of the Lord's Supper (*Missa ad Vesperum*), but the first has disappeared from use. It was the occasion for the public reconciliation of penitents (*Ordo agentibus publicam poenitentiam*) the ejection of whom, *cum lacrymis*, as we have already noted, was a feature of the ancient Ash Wednesday rite[26]. The old English name for Maundy Thursday, 'Shere Thursday' may represent an echo of this custom, 'shere' being possibly an obsolete word meaning pure or clean[27]. If the first mass of Maundy Thursday has long since disappeared and the Rite for the Public Reconciliation of Penitents on this day has

gone from the *Pontificale Romanum*, the last day of Lent
remains an appropriate day for the Sacrament of Reconciliation and many may still wish to make their confession on
the very threshold of the solemn celebration of the mystery
of redemption. Today is indeed a day of reconciliation, for
the sign of the remission of our sins and of our reconciliation with God in the new covenant is the fraternal banquet
of the Lord's Supper. We should remember too that the
circumstances of today's celebration give particular emphasis to the role of the Eucharist as the sacrament of unity,
and that it is sin which disperses and divides and scatters
abroad the people of God (John 11:52). We tend to think of
penance as the most 'private' of all the sacraments, as
indeed in a sense it is, but, as we have already noted, it does
have a public and communal dimension[28]. Our sacramental
reconciliation with God and his Church on this day is as
fitting an adaptation of today's ancient ceremony as our
receiving of ashes on Ash Wednesday is of that day's former
rite[29]. Not everyone will be able to go to confession on
Maundy Thursday itself, but we can try to do so at some
time in Holy Week, preferably before the Mass of the Lord's
Supper rather than on Good Friday or Easter Eve. The
revised formula of absolution in the Roman rite underlines
the paschal character of this sacrament:

> God, the Father of mercies,
> through the death and resurrection of his Son
> has reconciled the world to himself
> and sent the Holy Spirit among us
> for the forgiveness of sins;
> through the ministry of the Church
> may God give you pardon and peace,
> and I absolve you from your sins
> in the name of the Father, and of the Son,
> and of the Holy Spirit.

The Church of England has not yet been able to give
synodical approval to a rite for the reconciliation of a
penitent but forms of absolution proposed in 1981 contained the same opening phrase. It is a matter for regret

that it has been omitted from the form contained in *LHWE*

If the reconciliation of penitents speaks to us of the sacrament of penance then the consecration of the holy oils performed by the bishop in his cathedral at the *Missa Chrismatis* (or *Chrismalis*) speaks to us particularly of the sacraments of baptism, confirmation, ordination and the anointing of the sick. Indeed, the sacraments of initiation, celebrated so appropriately in the early days of the Church at the Easter Vigil, required great quantities of Holy Oil – for the all-over pre-baptismal anointing of the neophytes with the Oil of the Catechumens and for their post-baptismal anointing with the Oil of Chrism. The nearest available day for the consecration of these oils by the Bishop was the Thursday in Holy Week, Good Friday being clearly out of the question and Easter Eve itself a eucharistic *dies non*; hence the second of the mass formulae for this day found in the Gelasian Sacramentary. But we can see more than a merely historical and practical justification for this practice when we realize that, in celebrating on this day the inauguration of the New Covenant in the institution of the Eucharist, the Church is celebrating the mystery from which all the other sacraments take their origin and towards which they are all directed – the mystery of the Body of Christ, which is at the same time the mystery of the Church and the mystery of the Eucharist. Hence in the celebration of the Chrism Mass as reformed in the Roman rite there are two centres of interest: holy order, seen in its proper context of the priestly nature of the whole People of God, and the consecration of the holy oils which are at the service, as it were, of the priestly and sacramental ministry of the Church.

The celebration of the Chrism Mass should be seen as one of the most important diocesan occasions of the year and thus take place at a time and, if not in the cathedral, at a place convenient for the greatest possible number of priests and people. The new rite is a celebration of the common priesthood in Christ in which the bishop and his priests share and so it is important that the diocesan clergy are present in truly representative numbers to concelebrate with their bishop and to renew their priestly commitment. By celebrating this eucharist with their bishop the clergy and people give real expression to the unity which binds together the many separate celebrations in parishes and other communities throughout the diocese. The ministerial priesthood is an essential part of the royal priesthood of all the baptized, which it exists to serve and enable. Therefore this celebration should not be allowed to become an exclusively clerical occasion, as is made clear in the Introductory Sentence in the *ASB* proper (from Rev. 1:6) and even clearer in the proper preface of the Roman Rite:

> By your Holy Spirit you anointed your only Son High Priest of the new and eternal covenant. With wisdom and love you have planned that this one priesthood should continue in the Church.
> Christ gives the dignity of a royal priesthood to the people he has made his own. From these, with a brother's love, he chooses men to share his sacred ministry by the laying on of hands.
> He appoints them to renew in his name the sacrifice of our redemption as they set before your family his paschal meal. He calls them to lead your holy people in love, nourish them by your word, and strengthen them through the sacraments.
> Father, they are to give their lives in your service and for the salvation of your people as they strive to grow in the likeness of Christ.

This new preface sums up an entirely new element in the Chrism Mass, introduced in the reforms of Paul VI: the renewal of priestly commitment to Christ and to the service of his body, the Church. This takes place after the homily which, it is directed, should be preached by the bishop and which should "urge the priests to be faithful in fulfilling their office in the Church."

The second element in the Chrism Mass, the consecration of the holy oils for use throughout the diocese in the year ahead, is accomplished in a splendid ceremony furnished with texts and chants of great richness. The oils, carried into the presence of the bishop by three deacons, are blessed with formulae which clearly indicate the purposes for which they are to be used[30]. First comes the blessing of the Oil for the Sick as a medicine for the healing 'of body and soul'. The power of Christ should be seen as active in the anointing of the sick, making present and real for them the healing he practised when here on earth. The Oil of Catechumens, formerly called the Oil of Exorcism, is blessed next for use before baptism. The prayer askes for the gifts of wisdom, strength and understanding for those who are to be baptized. Finally, the Oil of Chrism, mixed with fragrant oil of flowers, is consecrated to be used at ordinations and in the sacraments of initiation. It is the oil of priesthood, both general – for those incorporated into Christ's priestly people at baptism – and particular – for those ordained to share in the ministerial priesthood of Christ – and those priests present and concelebrating with the bishop extend their hands for this prayer.

For those unable to be present at the Chrism Mass, the significance and importance of the Holy Oils could perhaps be emphasized by a rite of reception of the oils into the parish church at some suitable time.

## THE PASCHAL TRIDUUM

The reform of the liturgical year in the Roman rite has given a uniquely privileged place to the Three Days (or *Triduum*) of the Christian paschal celebration:

> Christ redeemed mankind and gave perfect glory to God principally through his paschal mystery: by dying he destroyed our death and by rising he restored our life. The Easter Triduum of the passion and resurrection of Christ is thus the culmination of the entire liturgical year. What Sunday is to the week, the solemnity of Easter is to the liturgical year.
> The Easter triduum begins with the evening Mass of the Lord's Supper, reaches its high point in the Easter Vigil, and closes with evening prayer on Easter Sunday.[31]

The provisions of *LHWE* make a similar point, with less precision however, in the introduction to the Maundy

Thursday evening eucharist. Although the word *triduum* does
not appear (it did figure in the first draft, but it was pointed
out in General Synod that it would need to be explained and
so was dropped), it is replaced by the word *continuum*:

> Maundy Thursday marks a new beginning, the beginning
> of the end. From this point on, our Christian worship is
> a continuum through to Easter morning. The Jewish
> beginning of the day (in the evening) unites the events of
> Maundy Thursday with the death of Christ the next
> afternoon.[32]

It is important however to bear in mind at this point that
though the term *triduum* is of great antiquity its exact application has varied. The significance attached to 'three days' and
'the third day' goes back to the New Testament[32a], the Creeds
and the earliest Christian tradition. Words are attributed to our
Lord in the Gospels which bring together his passion, death
and resurrection:

> Look, we are going up to Jerusalem, and the Son of man
> is about to be handed over to the chief priests and
> scribes. They will condemn him to death and will hand
> him over to the gentiles to be mocked and scourged and
> crucified; and on the third day he will be raised up again.
> (Matthew 20:18–19)

We have seen earlier that at first the Great Vigil was the
unitive celebration of Christ's passion and resurrection with no
separate commemoration on the days preceding it; it was
however preceded by the strict paschal fast of one or two
days, with priority given to the Saturday rather than the
Friday. The two day fast before the Night of Easter already
gives us a triduum – Friday, Saturday and Sunday; so S.Amb-
rose can speak of "the sacred triduum (*triduum illud sacrum*)
within which he suffered, lay in the tomb, and arose, the three
days of which he said: 'Destroy this temple and in three days
I will raise it up' "[33], and S.Augustine (whom S.Ambrose
baptized at Milan during the Easter Vigil in 387) can similarly
write of "the most holy triduum of the crucified, entombed
and risen one" (*sacratissimum triduum crucifixi, sepulti,
resuscitati*)[34]. It was not so much the introduction of the

distinct celebrations of Maundy Thursday and Good Friday which broke the unity of the Sacred Triduum as the later displacement of the proper times of their celebration; the moving of the Mass of the Lord's Supper to Thursday morning and, even more fatally serious, the shifting of the Great Vigil of Easter to the morning of Holy Saturday, with the consequent anticipation on the previous evening of Matins and Lauds (*Tenebrae*) of Thursday, Friday and Saturday. This involved a loss of the sense of chronological authenticity, what the Second Vatican Council called *veritas temporis*,[35] and led to the *Triduum Sacrum* being reckoned as the last three days of Holy Week; Thursday, Friday and Saturday. In theory this still included the celebration of the Resurrection, but the inclusion was far from evident and the unifying factor of the night and day of Easter being both part of the Triduum and of the Great Fifty Days was lost. The Triduum was seen more as a preparation for Easter than as embracing Easter, more as a Triduum of the Passion than as the Paschal Triduum.

There is an element of innovation in Paul VI's reform – both in the use of the title Paschal (or Easter) Triduum and in its beginning now with the Mass of the Lord's Supper on Thursday evening – but in the profoundest sense it marks a return to the principle expressed in the ancient *Triduum*. The same reform also specifies that Lent comes to an end on Maundy Thursday before the ushering in of the Easter *Triduum*. The new Triduum is indeed a continuum; although each day has its distinct emphasis, yet it is the Paschal Mystery in its unity that is celebrated, as we shall see, throughout.

## MAUNDY THURSDAY EVENING – THE SUPPER OF THE LORD

The Paschal Triduum now begins with the Evening Mass of the Lord's Supper. Outwardly it is a celebration of the Eucharist which (despite certain ceremonies peculiar to this one evening) is much like any other, but one that does succeed in expressing with particular force certain aspects of the eucharistic mystery which are not always so evident in other celebrations. It is clearly a joyful and festive

assembly of the People of God around the Table of the
Lord. Today the multiplication of celebrations is discouraged and masses without a congregation forbidden,
and – with the exception of the Chrism Mass – there should
normally be only one Mass, sung and with a sermon, in
every church. The bishop or the parish priest or the senior
priest of the community should preside "with the full
participation of the whole local community and with all the
priests and clergy exercising their ministry" as the rubrics
of the Roman rite express it. During this celebration
moreover the regrettable custom, strongly discouraged in
the *General Instruction* of the Roman Missal, of giving
Holy Communion from the Reserved Sacrament rather
than from hosts consecrated there and then at the Mass is
expressly forbidden: the tabernacle, pyx or aumbry is
already empty and the Blessed Sacrament has been
removed to a 'remote place' where it will remain until after
the Easter Vigil.

The themes of the celebration are indicated in the rubric
after the Gospel in the Roman rite: "The homily should
explain the principal mysteries which are commemorated in
this Mass: the institution of the eucharist, the institution of
the priesthood, and Christ's commandment of brotherly
love." It perhaps needs to be said at this point that most
Anglicans would probably feel uneasy about this reference
to "the institution of the priesthood". The Last Supper is
emphatically not seen in the best theology today (of any
tradition) as the occasion of the 'ordination' of the Twelve
to the priesthood by virtue of the command our Lord, "Do
this in remembrance of me." The rubric however does not
commit us to any such theology; it only commits us to the
kind of link between eucharist and priesthood which is
expressed in the *Final Report* of ARCIC:

> Because the eucharist is the memorial of the sacrifice
> of Christ, the action of the presiding minister in
> reciting again the words of Christ at the last supper
> and distributing to the assembly the holy gifts is seen
> to stand in a sacramental relation to what Christ
> himself did in offering his own sacrifice. So our two

traditions commonly use priestly terms in speaking about the ordained ministry.[36]

Before we go on to speak of the two other themes of the Lord's Supper and the Footwashing there is one other theme, less prominent today than formerly but nevertheless still present, which deserves some comment. It would seem that an ancient name for today is 'the day of the tradition'[37] and both *traditio* in the Latin and *paradosis* in the Greek of the New Testament have a double meaning. In the context of tonight's celebration they refer both to Christ's *handing over* of his life to the Father and *passing on* his Body and Blood to his Church and to his being *handed over* to his enemies by Judas[38]. Formerly there was a reference to Judas in the Collect of the Roman rite and the kiss of peace was omitted because of the kiss of Judas; today it is only in the Eastern rite that Judas is mentioned (except in the Gospel reading) in a thrice repeated *troparion*:

Receive me today, O Son of God,
as a partaker of thy Mystic Feast;
for I will not speak of the Mystery to thine enemies;
I will not kiss thee as did Judas;
but as a thief I will confess thee:
Lord, remember me when thou comest in thy
    Kingdom.[39]

In the modern Roman rite the Collect speaks of the Supper which Christ left to his Church "when he was about to die" (*morti se traditurus*); the second Reading (found also in Anglican rites) from the First Letter to the Corinthians makes clear the double meaning of *paradosis-traditio* when S.Paul speaks of *handing on* what he had received and goes on to speak of the night on which he was betrayed or, more properly, *handed over*; a clause added on this one occasion to the First Eucharistic Prayer refers to the day when "our Lord was betrayed for us" (*pro nobis est traditus*, again - more properly - "was handed over for us"); finally, the Communion antiphon in its Latin original, quoting the Old Vulgate of I Corinthians 11:24, speaks of the Body of Christ *handed over* for us (*tradetur*).

The dominant theme tonight, however, is the Supper of the Lord, but the Supper seen not exclusively as the institution of the Eucharist but experienced in the context of a paschal celebration which cannot but embrace the whole mystery of redemption. The Roman entrance antiphon gives this wider context: "We should glory in the cross of our Lord Jesus Christ, for he is our salvation, our life and our resurrection; through him we are saved and set free." The paschal background is emphasized by the first reading (identical in the Roman rite and *LHWE*) from the 12th chapter of Exodus; instructions for the Passover meal. It is the themes of the Supper and the Eucharist which dominate the Collect, the first two readings and responsorial psalm, the Proper Preface, the Communion Antiphon and the Postcommunion prayers in both rites and the words adapted from the Jewish passover meal which introduce the Preparation of the Gifts in *LHWE*[40]. Above all, of course, there is the fact that the way in which we give thanks for the gift of the Eucharist is by making eucharist; we not only remember the Supper, we celebrate it.

The remaining theme, Christ's commandment of brotherly love, is the theme of the Gospel, which, in both rites, is the story from the 13th chapter of John of the washing of the disciples' feet by our Lord. This may be followed, after the sermon, by the ceremony of the Washing of Feet. Many hesitate to introduce this ceremony, fearing that it will seem unreal, theatrical, embarrassing: few parishes, however, once they have taken the plunge, will ever want to go back on it. It is experienced as a powerful and moving, though down to earth, act of service. Nevertheless, both the Gospel reading and the ceremony seem to many to introduce into this liturgy a new and puzzlingly different, even distracting, theme.

The Fourth Gospel, for some mysterious reason, does not mention the institution of the Eucharist in its narrative of the Last Supper. In its place we find a story which none of the other gospels record, the narrative of the footwashing. It is not that John is ignorant of the tradition that our Lord instituted the eucharist on this night, or unaware of the familiarity of his readers with that tradition. He is in no way anti-sacramental, for although he omits any reference to the institution of either Baptism or the Eucharist, his gospel is full of allusions to both, and his whole approach to the mystery of Christ is deeply sacramental. And if the Church has chosen this passage to be the liturgical gospel for tonight it is because this story complements – and in no way contradicts – the reading from S.Paul about the institution of the Eucharist.

The washing of the disciples' feet is a sign which, as we have come to expect from the Fourth Gospel, has more that one level of meaning and interpretation. At one level it is a reminder that Christ came among us as a *Servant*, and that we are called to live and act as servants of one another in a Christ-like manner. At another level it is a reference to Baptism: "If I do not wash you, you can have no share with me" (John 13:8). We are clearly here beyond the level of a moral lesson about mutual love and service; we are here dealing with the cleansing power of Christ's sacrificial death upon the cross, to which the footwashing points, applied to us through the waters of baptism[41]. At a deeper level still we are in the presence of one who discloses his essential identity as one "who, being in the form of God, did not count equality with God something to be grasped. But he emptied himself, taking the form of a slave . . . he was humbler yet, even to accepting death, death on a cross" (Philippians 2:6-8).

To discover how the footwashing story casts light upon the Eucharist we must take our start from the traditional English name for today – *Maundy* Thursday[42]. This is derived from the Latin *mandatum novum*, meaning a new commandment. "I give you a *new commandment*:" says Jesus later in the same chapter of John, "love one another; you must love one another just as I have loved you." (John 13:34). And it is this new commandment which is the unifying theme of this Mass of the Lord's Supper, of this opening rite of the *Triduum Sacrum*. For the mystery celebrated tonight and throughout the whole *Triduum* is supremely one of love; it is about total, sacrificial, self-giving love. On this night Jesus Christ gave himself in total self-giving love to the Father and in total self-giving love to his fellow men. This handing over of his life to death is signified by Jesus by his words and actions over the bread and the cup, but so too is the double movement of his offering – *to* God and *for* mankind. He gives thanks to his Father over the bread and the cup, but he also addresses his disciples. His body is *for* them, the new covenant in his blood is *for* them. Nothing is withheld of love and obedience from the Father; nothing is withheld of love and service from mankind. The gift is total, free, and unconditional; he loves "to the end" (John 13:1).

The double movement of love is also an essential aspect of the eucharistic mystery. In the eucharist we are taken up into the movement of Christ's own self-offering to the Father, and at the same time are renewed in our commitment to one another in the common life of the Body of Christ. For we *are* the Body of Christ and in receiving Holy Communion, as S.Augustine reminds us, we say *Amen* to the mystery we have become[43]. Again, as the *Final Report* of ARCIC reminds us in its discussion of that pregnant Greek word *koinonia* which means communion, fellowship, participation in a common life, "koinonia with one another is entailed by our koinonia with God in Christ. This is the mystery of the Church"[44]. In this particular Maundy Thursday celebration of the Eucharist (and, by extension, in every other celebration of the Eucharist) we are intimately involved in the double movement of the love of Christ. We are called to respond to a double challenge: can we refuse the *mandatum novum* of brotherly love, can we refuse to share the peace of Christ, can we refuse to wash one another's feet? And can we refuse to be taken up by Christ and offered with him to the Father? Both are costly, risky and dangerous: we can refuse both but we cannot accept the one without the other. Holy Communion – Holy *koinonia* – is communion with God in Christ and communion with one another.

In the Rule of S.Benedict a whole chapter, chapter 53, is devoted to the reception of guests in the monastery. Benedict writes:

All guests who present themselves are to be welcomed as Christ, for he himself will say: 'I was a stranger and

you welcomed me' (Matthew 25:35). Proper honour
must be be shown 'to all, especially to those who share
our faith' (Galatians 6:10) and to pilgrims... All
humility should be shown in addressing a guest on
arrival or departure. By a bow of the head or by a
complete prostration of the body, Christ is to be adored
because he is indeed welcomed in them... The abbot
shall pour water on the hands of the guests, and the
abbot with the entire community, shall wash their
feet... Great care and concern are to be shown in
receiving poor people and pilgrims, because in them
more particularly Christ is received.[45]

The hymn *Ubi caritas et amor*, suggested for use during the
footwashing by *LHWE* (in note 3) and for use at the
offertory procession in the Roman rite, was in fact
composed for use at the footwashing in the Benedictine
Abbey of Reichenau in about AD.800 [46]. The Latin words
will be familiar to many through the beautiful arrangement
of the traditional plainsong by Maurice Duruflé; a fine
English version with words by James Quinn, S.J., can be
found in the *New English Hymnal* at 513.

It must be a matter for real regret that the Roman rite,
unlike *LHWE*, does not include verses 27 to 29 in its
second Reading from I Corinthians 11 tonight, for the
real key to the link between the Footwashing and the
Eucharist is surely S.Paul's warning about receiving the
Blessed Sacrament unworthily when we fail to "discern
the Lord's Body" (I Corinthians 11:29 NEB)[47]. Certainly
we fail to discern the Lord's Body when we fail to discern
in the consecrated bread the true Body of Christ, but we
fail no less to discern the Lord's Body when we fail to
discern in our brothers and sisters, our fellow members of
the Body, the real presence of Christ. As C.S.Lewis
reminds us:

Next to the Blessed Sacrament itself, your neighbour is
the holiest object presented to your senses. If he is your
Christian neighbour he is holy in almost the same way,
for in him also Christ... is truly hidden.[48]

The same point was made with greater force by Frank Weston, Bishop of Zanzibar, in a speech delivered to the Anglo-Catholic Congress of 1923, when he pointed out to Anglicans:

> You have got your Mass, you have got your Altar, you have begun to get your Tabernacle. Now go out into the highways and hedges ... Go out and look for Jesus in the ragged, in the naked, in the oppressed and sweated, in those who have lost hope, in those who are struggling to make good. Look for Jesus. And when you see him, gird yourselves with his towel and try to wash their feet.[49]

After the Last Supper came the Agony in the Garden of Gethsemane. So from the beginning of the particular observance of Maundy Thursday there has been a strong instinct to prolong the Eucharist by a watch of prayer. As J.T.Martin has written:

> It is the night of Gethsemane, of our Lord's agonized prayer, of Judas's kiss, of the arrest; the night of the trial before the Sanhedrin, and of Peter's triple denial before cockcrow. Jesus did not sleep this night, and his disciples only fitfully, for he did not hesitate to rouse them from their slumbers – *Watch and pray*. There is severity in his voice when he comes to them the third time and asks, 'Are you still sleeping and taking your rest?' (Mark 14.41). He seems particularly to have required companionship on this night.[50]

We have already seen from Egeria's account how the night between Maundy Thursday and Good Friday was observed in the fourth-century Jerusalem Church; we have also seen how in the Byzantine tradition there is today a watch of prayer on this night in the Eastern manner. In the West a particular significance has gathered around this watch because of the need to give Holy Communion on Good Friday from the Sacrament consecrated today, a need which is discussed below in the section on Good Friday. In what is now described the detailed provisions of the Roman rite are followed, but it should be noted that *LHWE* does from the celebration of the Sacraments on those two days[56].

It is for this reason that the Byzantine liturgy which provides for the Liturgy of the Presanctified (a public distribution of communion from the Reserved Sacrament after Vespers) on the weekdays of Lent makes no such provision on Good Friday; the fast is not even broken by the reception of Holy Communion.[57] This primitive rule has also been maintained in the Church of Milan; the Ambrosian rite provides only for a Liturgy of the Word and the Veneration of the Cross[58]. For a long time the same rule was observed in Rome and even when provison for Holy Communion from the Reserved Sacrament (at first in both kinds) began to be made in order to meet the pressure of popular devotion, the Pope and his deacons at first made a point of abstaining. In the later Middle Ages the situation was reversed, when, in the time of Innocent III, it was the Pope alone who made his communion. In 1953, after the restoration of the nocturnal Easter Vigil in 1951, an International Liturgical Congress was held in Lugano to prepare for the promulgation of the revised Order for Holy Week of 1955. The experts were divided as to what solution should be proposed for Good Friday, though all agreed that there was no justification for the celebrant alone communicating and that the confusing ceremonies of the Mass of the Presanctified could not be continued. Dom Bernard Capelle argued for a general communion; Fr Jungmann and Professor Fischer wanted to abolish communion altogether, pointing to the usage of Milan. It was Capelle's view that prevailed.

Some Anglicans have argued in favour of a full eucharistic celebration on Good Friday, and *LHWE* allows for three possibilities; a celebration of the Eucharist, a distribution of Holy Communion from the Reserved Sacrament, or an Antecommunion only, although it strongly encourages the reception of Holy Communion. One motive leading Anglicans to press for a Good Friday eucharist has been doubt as to the legitimacy of general communion from the Reserved Sacrament, though there can be no doubt that this practice

allow for exactly the same observance (in somewhat hermetic language in introductory notes 6 and 7 to Maundy Thursday and note 38 in the rite itself and somewhat more clearly in the introduction to Good Friday). The eucharistic celebration concludes with the prayer after communion and a solemn procession with cross, lights and incense is formed to accompany the Blessed Sacrament, carried by the principal celebrant, to a specially prepared altar (the Altar of Repose), while the great eucharistic hymn of S. Thomas Aquinas, *Pange lingua gloriosa corporis mysterium* [51] is sung. The Altar of Repose is specially, but soberly, decorated with lights and flowers and situated in a side chapel which will provide the venue for a watch of prayer at least until midnight. Meanwhile the High Altar and sanctuary are stripped so that the altar is left completely bare and any crosses which cannot be removed are veiled.

There is a two-fold character to this watch on Maundy Thursday evening. It is of course a watch before the Blessed Sacrament and therefore has the character of a prolonged meditation upon and thanksgiving for the great gift of the Eucharist instituted on this night. Abuses, however, are guarded against. The recent letter of the Congregation for Divine Worship on *Celebrating Easter* underlines the fact that the Altar of Repose serves for Good Friday communion by insisting that this "transfer of the Blessed Sacrament may not be carried out if the Liturgy of the Lord's Passion will not be celebrated in that same Church on the following day"; it also makes clear that the Sacrament is to be reserved in a closed tabernacle or pyx and under no circumstances exposed in a monstrance[52]. Moreover the candles and flowers put out to honour the Blessed Sacrament are to be removed at midnight even if the watch itself continues right through the night. But, secondly, the Watch of Prayer has gathered around it all the events which the Gospel narratives associate with this night. It can and should take place even if the Blessed Sacrament is not being reserved at the Altar of Repose and it should commemorate all the events of this sacred night. Parishes may well want to establish a rhythm, with long periods of silent adoration punctuated by readings from the Gospels and corporately led prayer and meditation. *Celebrating Easter* recommends readings from S.John's Gospel, chapters 13 – 17; *LHWE* provides for readings from these same chapters with accompanying psalms and a Gospel of the Watch (Luke 22:31–62 in Year A; Matthew 26:30-end in Year B; Mark 14:26-end in Year C). The emphasis upon the Watch is dictated not only by the chronology of the Passion and the need to watch with Christ at least one hour on the night of his agony but also by the need to underline the unity and continuity which bind together Maundy Thursday and Good Friday, the Supper and the Cross.

## GOOD FRIDAY

Until recently – and still up to a point today – the Church's liturgy has been far from providing a unanimous focus for the devotion of the Christian people on this day in Western Christendom. Neither the unreformed Roman rite, the so-called Mass of the Pre-sanctified, celebrated on Friday morning in Latin and with the reception of Holy Communion confined to the celebrant, nor the more austere Prayer Book provision of Mattins, Litany, Antecommunion and Evensong were found to be adequate channels of popular devotion. Because on the whole the People of God were not being fed by the liturgy the gap was filled with non-liturgical services of various kinds, particularly in the Roman Catholic Church with Stations of the Cross and in both our traditions with the preaching of the Three Hours' Devotion, a service which has enjoyed a surprising popularity in the Church of England considering that it originated with the Jesuits in Peru towards the end of the seventeenth century[53]. Although many of these non-liturgical devotions – including in our own day ecumenical acts of witness – have proved of immense value to countless Christians, they have lacked the objective and corporate character which only liturgical worship can give. There is moreover on this day of all days a need for liturgical *action*; for the Church needs not only to hear and ponder the Word of the Cross and render the verbal homage of love and faith and penitence, but also to express in concrete liturgical action

her response to the divine initiative in the Cross an union with it. So the first claim upon us on Good F must always be the liturgy of the day; nothing mu allowed to challenge that priority[54].

The restored Celebration of the Lord's Passion fall three main sections; it is the combination into one of rites which were originally distinct and not necess celebrated in the order in which we now find them. Th first of all the *Synaxis* or Liturgy of the Word, conclu with the Solemn Prayers or General Intercession. Th followed by the Veneration of the Cross, a rite which cl proclaims its oriental origin, deriving as we have seen the fourth-century Jerusalem usage, described by Eger venerating the relic of the True Cross at Golgotha. The section is the rite of Holy Communion from the Rese Sacrament, for which hosts consecrated on Maundy Th day are used. This liturgy is to take place in the aftern about three o'clock, unless pastoral reasons suggest a hour.

The most important of the reforms introduced into rite in 1955 was the restoration of a general commun the unrevised rite of the Mass of the Presanctified confusing title, at best, since the Mass is not celebra had since 1622 allowed only for the communion of celebrant. The historical background is complex and for some explanation. It is well known that the unbro Catholic tradition of both East and West has ne admitted a eucharistic celebration on Good Friday and t the same held true of Holy Saturday until the Mass of Easter Vigil came in the West to be anticipated first Saturday evening and finally in the morning[55]. An e earlier tradition, however, extended this abstinence to reception of Holy Communion, as is made clear in a fam letter from Pope Innocent I (AD 401–417) to Decentius

It is quite clear that the Apostles during these two days both were in mourning and also hid themselve from the Jews. And further there is no doubt they fasted on the aforesaid two days to such a degree that the tradition of the Church requires entire abstinenc

is not only ancient but ecumenical. It derives from the primitive practice of the faithful taking the sacrament to their homes at the end of the Sunday eucharist in order to communicate themselves at home during the week, which then moved to church and was given an organized liturgical structure in the Byzantine rite earlier than in the Roman rite. Communion from the Reserved Sacrament has moreover from pre-Nicene days been normally in one kind only and this cannot be said to weaken the the Anglican principle of insisting on communion in both kinds being distributed at the eucharist. Indeed on this occasion there is perhaps no reason why the Sacrament cannot be reserved in both kinds and this would be a return to the former Roman usage as described in the Gelasian Sacramentary.

Another motive behind Anglican arguments for a Good Friday eucharist has been the appeal to post-Reformation Anglican history. There is evidence that the Eucharist was celebrated on this day in some places in the seventeenth century and probably more frequently in the eighteenth and early nineteenth centuries[59]. The exclusive concentration of the Prayer Book Consecration Prayer on the Passion of our Lord and the generalized Protestant view of the time that the Lord's Supper was a privileged way of remembering the Lord's death favoured the practice (although it was also to be found amongst the High Churchmen of the time). The practice went into a decline in the later nineteenth century under Tractarian influence, which led to the desire to return to Catholic tradition and to a fuller and richer eucharistic theology.

Many Anglicans however, while conscious of the liturgical arguments against a Good Friday eucharist, would argue that there are no real theological reasons against it. In order to appreciate the profound theological insight behind the traditional Catholic rule it is necessary to set Good Friday in the closest possible association with Maundy Thursday and with the Easter Vigil. It is no mere historical accident that Holy Communion is given on Good Friday from the Sacrament consecrated on Maundy Thursday evening. Egeria witnesses to the fact that in fourth-century Jerusalem Thursday and Friday constituted a single celebration of unbroken unity. "For a doctrinal reason of supreme appropriateness the Church of Jerusalem celebrated the Supper of the Lord on Thursday at Calvary in order to demonstrate the unity of the eucharistic sacrifice and that of the Cross"[60]. The Supper and the Cross are so closely linked that they form a single act of sacrifice and cannot be understood without reference to each other. The Cross gives meaning to the Supper, but the Supper also gives meaning to the Cross. In the provisions of the liturgy we see, writes Louis Bouyer,

> a striking symbol of the truth ... upon which everything in these varied ceremonies depends: the Cross of Christ is not defeat but victory, because that which gives it its true meaning is not the execution accomplished by the Jews on Friday but the offering Jesus made of himself at the Last Supper on Holy Thursday[61].

Our paschal celebration within the Easter Triduum is, and should be seen to be, essentially indivisible. If we do not celebrate the eucharist on Good Friday it is in part because we are waiting to give thanks for the Cross until we can give thanks for it together with the Resurrection in the one great unitive eucharistic celebration of the Easter Vigil. Anglicans sometimes need to be reminded themselves that every eucharist is as much a proclamation of the resurrection as a memorial of the Cross.

If we turn to look at the three sections of the Good Friday Liturgy we find that the first, the Synaxis, is of the simplest and most austere character. The silent procession into the church and prostration of the ministers before the stripped and bare altar and the solemn singing of the Passion do make a dramatic impact, but the emotion is restrained and the emphasis is concentrated on the word. In this meditative dialogue we feed upon God's word and respond in faith, in words themselves provided by Scripture. The first two readings provided in the present Roman Rite are Isaiah 52:13 – 53:12 with part of Psalm 31 and Hebrews 4:14-16, 5:7-9 with a chant from Philipians 2. *LHWE* provides the same reading from Isaiah but with part of Psalm 22 and either the same reading from Hebrews or a part of Hebrews 10. There is some evidence that the lessons from Hosea 6 and Exodus 12 in the former Roman rite together with the Johannine narrative of the Passion and Resurrection were used at the Easter Vigil in the pre-Nicene period at Rome before there was any liturgy of the word on Good Friday[62].

It is no mere historical accident either that reserves the Passion according to John for the liturgy of Good Friday, for it is the Johannine account that stresses the victory of the Cross and paints for us a picture of *Christus regnans in cruce*. Michael Ramsey has written:

> In the Passion story of S.John the glory dominates. In the garden the soldiers fall to the ground awestruck (18:6). In the judgement hall Pilate is the broken prisoner and Jesus is the judge (18:33–38). Majestically Jesus carries his own cross to Calvary, going where he wills to go as one who has power to lay down his life (cf 10:17–18). Before he dies he cries that the divine purpose is accomplished (19:30), and he entrusts his own spirit to the Father (ibid.). Dying as the king, Jesus is no less the Passover lamb. Pilate delivers him to die at the moment when the lambs are being prepared for sacrifice (19:14). The king and the sacrificial victim are one Christ. Thus the Johannine story of the Passion both reflects and creates the imagery in the Church of One who is both lamb and king, victim and conqueror. *Vexilla regis prodeunt* - "The royal banners forward go".[63].

Commenting on the recent restoration of the reading of the Johannine Passion on Good Friday in the American Lutheran *Book of Worship*, the Lutheran theologian, Krister Stendahl, can make a similar point from another angle:

> The majestic death of Jesus according to the Gospel of John reminds us of earlier Christian art. Long before there were crucifixes with the suffering Jesus, plagued by the crown of thorns, the Jesus of Bernard of Clairvaux and Paul Gerhard [the seventeenth-century

German author of the hymn *O Sacred head, sore
wounded . . . NEH* 90] there was the triumphal crucifix
with the victorious Jesus standing in royal and priestly
garb, hands outstretched in the blessing embrace of the
world."[64]

In the sermon which follows the reading of the Passion the
preacher should bear in mind the warning of another distinguished Lutheran theologian, the Swedish bishop, Gustaf
Aulén:

Good Friday appears in its right perspective only when
it is seen in the light of Easter. If the note of triumph is
not present in preaching on the passion, this preaching
has lost its Christian character.[65]

The ministry of the Word has, as it were, placarded the
cross of Christ before our minds and imaginations. After this
we are to unite our wills to the will of him who "opened
wide his arms for us on the Cross"[66] by joining in intercession for the needs of the Church and the World. As the
opening monition in the new American Prayer Book puts it:

Our heavenly Father sent his Son into the world, not to
condemn the world, but that the world through him
might be saved; that all who believe in him might be
delivered from the power of sin and death, and become
heirs with him of everlasting life. We pray, therefore, for
people everywhere according to their needs.

The Solemn Prayers (whose origins are of great antiquity) are
an impressive exercise in corporate intercession: first a
bidding, then the congregation's silent prayer, then a collect
recited by the celebrant, whose outstretched arms may serve
to remind us of the arms of Christ stretched out upon the
cross in order to draw and embrace all humanity to himself.[67]

We move now to the most dramatic section of the liturgy,
the Veneration of the Cross, and we cannot help noticing the
change of style from the sober and restrained austerity of
Roman *gravitas* to a mood of vivid, poignant, eloquent
emotion. In this creative Franco-Germanic reworking of the

fourth-century Jerusalem rite, which we owe to the ninth and tenth centuries, the Cross of Christ is no longer placarded only before our minds and hearts and wills; now it is right in front of our eyes that we have "a clear picture of Jesus Christ crucified" (Galatians 3:1) and that God's people "look on the one whom they have pierced" (John 19:37 and Zechariah 12:10). A crucifix is brought to the sanctuary escorted by lighted candles; it is solemnly held up before the people inviting their response of worship, and then all come – celebrant, ministers, congregation – to kneel before the cross and kiss it. There is no idolatry in this kiss; we hardly need to be reminded so soon after celebrating the twelfth centenary of the Second Council of Nicaea (AD 787) that in the veneration of an icon the honour paid to the image passes to its prototype. But neither is this kiss a light matter either, especially when we take to heart all that is implied in so simple a gesture.

To embrace the Cross is to make an act of faith in Christ and his Cross, an act of faith that is also an act of gratitude, of penitence and of love. In the *Reproaches* (*Improperia*), which are sung during the Veneration and which, inspired by Scripture (eg Micah 6:3-4), seem to be of Gallican or Spanish origin, Christ himself in dialogue with his faithless people challenges us to make this response: "My people, what have I done to you? How have I offended you? Answer me!" Our reply – in the words of the Greek *Trisagion* is both an act of faith and a call for mercy: *Hagios o Theos, Sanctus Deus; Hagios Ischyros, Sanctus Fortis; Hagios Athanatos, eleison himas, Sanctus Immortalis, miserere nobis* (Holy God, Holy and Mighty, Holy and Immortal, have mercy upon us). The embrace is also a welcoming of the Cross into our lives; we welcome it as the tree of life but knowing it also to be an instrument of death and shame, which Christ himself endured for the joy that was set before him. We too must be ready to endure the weight and shame of the Cross at some very real cost to ourselves; we have soberly and lucidly to recognize this as we embrace the Cross with a kiss. We have made our pledge and we cannot complain if we are then called upon to honour it. Our glorification of the Cross on Good Friday subtracts nothing from its realism.

In the Veneration we pay our homage not to a corpse but to a reigning sovereign. The whole ceremony is performed in the light of the Johannine presentation of the Gospel: the Cross is held up erect and candles burn on either side. For the Cross is a throne as well as an altar and we are taking part in the Homage at a Coronation. In the English Coronation Rite those who do homage go up to the throne, kneel and swear allegiance and then kiss the sovereign's cheek or hand. There is a clear analogy here with what we are doing on Good Friday. Our kiss must be that of a faithful subject, not that of the traitor Judas.

The traditional text of the Reproaches was attacked by the former Bishop of Birmingham, Dr Hugh Montefiore, in the General Synod debate on the Holy Week liturgy on the 13th February 1985 on the grounds that it was antisemitic; the 1986 *LHWE* therefore now contains an entirely new text, which may or may not survive the test of time. There is no doubt that many Anglicans will continue to use the traditional text, as found in the Roman order or in the *New English Hymnal* (516). Properly understood, there is nothing antisemitic about the Reproaches. In this text, as in the *Exsultet* ("This is the night when first you saved our fathers"), an identity is claimed between the People of God of the Old Covenant and the People of God of the New; in the Reproaches our Lord is engaged in a dialogue with *us*, challenging those present at the liturgy to faith, love and repentance and reproaching us with examples of our infidelity taken from the past history of the People of God. As Pope Pius XI was to say in answer to Nazi antisemitism, "we are all spiritually Semites"; we are one with "our fathers" in an inheritance both of shame and of glory and we cannot claim one without the other. Alongside the Reproaches two other chants are provided which emphasize the glory and triumph of the Cross; they are the ninth-century antiphon *Crucem tuam* ('We worship you, Lord, we venerate your cross, we praise your resurrection. Through the cross you brought joy to the world') and the magnificent hymn of Venantius Fortunatus, *Pange lingua* (Sing, my tongue, the glorious battle) with its refrain *Crux fidelis* (Faithful Cross)[68].

The Rite of the Veneration of the Cross has inspired some of the greatest composers (such as Palestrina and Victoria) to write some of their finest music for today's liturgy; it is less well known that the same rite – or at least the same cultus – inspired the masterpiece with which the history of Christian poetry in England begins, the early eighth-century *Dream of the Rood*, which speaks of the Cross as a "most wondrous tree", "the tree of glory", "this ardent beacon", "The tree of a Ruler".

> . . . Then I saw Man's Lord
> Hasten with great courage, intent on climbing me.
> Durst I not then oppose the word of the Lord
> And bend or break, though I saw tremble
> The surface of earth. All those foes
> I could have felled, yet I stood firm.
> Then the young warrior – it was God Almighty –
> Stalwart, resolute, stripped himself; climbed the high
>     gallows
> Gallantly before the throng, resolved to loose man's
>     bonds.[69]

All this helps to remind us that the Cross unveils the love of God; we see there not only the sacrifice of the Man Jesus of Nazareth but the divine initiative coming close to us in redeeming love. "God was in Christ reconciling the world to himself" (2 Corinthians 5:19); "So it is proof of God's own love for us, that Christ died for us while we were yet sinners" (Romans 5:8). The Cross is only a challenge because it is first and foremost a gift, a liberation and a revelation.

It is because the strongest emphasis must rest on what God has done for us rather than on our response that we move on from the Veneration to the final section of the rite, the distribution of Holy Communion. The Blessed Sacrament is brought from the place of repose to the Altar and all say together the Lord's Prayer and receive Communion. The rite then concludes with a collect and a prayer over the people. Our closest union with Christ is a sacramental union; in Holy Communion he takes the initiative, entering

into our lives and bringing with him his life-giving Cross
and all the graces of his Passion.

> He endured the nails, the spitting,
> Vinegar and spear and reed;
> From that holy Body pierced
> Blood and water forth proceed:
> Earth and stars and sky and ocean
> By that flood from stain are freed.[70]

## HOLY SATURDAY

Holy Saturday or Easter Eve has its own unique character
and its own importance in the carefully balanced structure
of the Paschal Triduum. It has tended to be neglected,
partly because the pressure to anticipate the Easter Vigil
found in both the history of Eastern and Western Christendom meant that one passed almost directly from Good
Friday to Easter Day without the necessary and meaningful
pause of Holy Saturday; and partly because it has become a
day given over to decorating the church with flowers and, at
least until recently, to celebrating weddings. It has also been
neglected precisely because it is an 'aliturgical' day when
the eucharist is not celebrated. It is essentially a day of
waiting; a fast, but a fast kept in a spirit of quiet confidence
and joyful hope. "On Holy Saturday," the rubrics of the
Roman Order explain, "the Church waits at the Lord's
tomb, meditating on his suffering and death. The altar is
left bare and the sacrifice of the Mass is not celebrated."

In the Church of England, *LHWE* fortunately clarifies a
situation which was dangerously compromised by the
*Alternative Service Book's* provision of a Proper for Easter
Eve complete with a Proper Preface and Postcommunion
Sentence. It reminds us firmly that "according to ancient
custom there is no celebration of the eucharist on Easter
Eve. The orders of Morning and Evening Prayer offer
adequate liturgical provision for the day, though the
material on pages 570 – 572 of the *ASB* is suitable for a
service of Antecommunion. It is particularly important that
Evening Prayer should be treated, by the style of its

celebration, as belonging to the Eve, and not as the first service of Easter, anticipating the Easter liturgy itself"[71]. There has never been any provision for a Liturgy of the Word in the Roman Rite on this day but the Ambrosian Rite does provide for an Antecommunion with the same Gospel (Matthew 27:57-66) as that found in the Book of Common Prayer and the *Alternative Service Book*.

The Roman Office of Readings provides for today a reading "from an ancient homily for Holy Saturday" which powerfully evokes the unique character of this day and also reminds us of the traditional eastern Easter iconography of the Harrowing of Hell, fine examples of which are to be found in the former church of S.Saviour-in-Chora, Constantinople (The Karije Museum, Istanbul) and S.Mark's Basilica, Venice[72]. It begins:

What is happening? Today there is a great silence over the earth, a great silence, and stillness, a great silence because the King sleeps; the earth was in terror and was still,because God slept in the flesh and raised up those who were sleeping from the ages. God has died in the flesh, and the underworld has trembled.

Truly he goes to seek out our first parent like a lost sheep; he wishes to visit those who sit in darkness and in the shadow of death. He goes to free the prisoner Adam and his fellow-prisoner Eve from their pains, he who is God and Adam's son.

The Lord goes into them holding his victorious weapon, his cross. When Adam, the first created man, sees him, he strikes his breast in terror and cries out to all: 'My Lord be with you all.' And Christ in reply says to Adam: 'And with your spirit.' And grasping his hand he raises him up, saying, 'Awake, O sleeper, and arise from the dead, and Christ shall give you light.'

Whether the Anglican priest-poet George Herbert, familiar certainly with the works of many of the early Fathers, ever saw an Eastern icon of the Resurrection or the mosaics of Venice remains open to speculation[73]; nevertheless, in his poem *Easter* he too calls to mind the atmosphere both of this passage and of the *Anastasis* icon:

Rise heart, thy Lord is risen. Sing his praise
Without delayes.
*Who takes thee by the hand*, that thou likewise
With him mayst rise . . .

## THE EASTER VIGIL

If there is one essential characteristic of the Easter Vigil it is
that, like the Jewish Passover, it is a nocturnal celebration:
"The night when Yahweh kept vigil to bring them out of
Egypt must be kept as a vigil in honour of Yahweh by all
Israelites, for all generations." (Exodus 12:42). S.Augustine
can express the common mind of the Latin and Greek Fathers
when he exhorts his congregation:

> In exhorting us to imitate his example, S.Paul the
> Apostle, besides enumerating his many other outstanding
> virtues, mentions also that he often spent the night in
> watching (2 Corinthians 11:27). How much more assidu-
> ously, then, ought we to keep watch on this particular
> vigil, which is, we may say, the mother of all sacred
> vigils, when the entire world is committed to keeping a
> night watch . . . Therefore let us watch and pray, that
> both outwardly and inwardly we may celebrate this vigil.
> God speaks to us in the readings of his holy word. Let
> us speak to God in our prayers. If we listen in docility to
> his sayings, he whom we petition takes up his dwelling
> in our hearts.[74]

Yet it is precisely the question of the timing of the Vigil
today that presents many pastoral problems. It is no longer
what it originally was, an all-night vigil ending with the
Eucharist at cock-crow. While it is true that modern
congregations do not have the same appetite or endurance
for such vigils as their predecessors, yet it can hardly be
denied that unless the Vigil lasts for two hours at the very
least it fails to qualify for the name of a vigil, a watch.
*Celebrating Easter* reminds us sharply that the Vigil must
take place at night, beginning not before nightfall and
ending before daybreak, and condemns the abuse of

celebrating it too early "at the time of day it is customary to celebrate anticipated Sunday Masses"[75]. The symbolism of the new Fire and of the Paschal Candle needs to be taken seriously; it can only be fully respected and appreciated when the celebration takes place in darkness. Although there is a custom particularly associated with Germany of celebrating the Vigil in the early hours of the morning, in most places the Vigil will be timed to end at or shortly before midnight. *LHWE* has to face the fact that there will be resistance to the Vigil in many Anglican parishes and a desire to divide it in many others, and with some reluctance it makes provision accordingly. The ideal is clear; if possible the Easter Liturgy is to be celebrated as one unbroken whole, concluding with the Eucharist (which is not to be omitted "except for serious reason") at dawn or as late as possible during the night. If this is not possible, it suggests holding an extended Liturgy of the Word, which it calls the Vigil, on Saturday evening and moving the Service of Light and the Baptismal Liturgy to a eucharistic celebration on Sunday morning. This rather makes a nonsense of the *Exsultet*, as to sing it in daylight can hardly be said to respect the language of the text. Since all these concessions and compromises will be found to be inevitably unsatisfactory, priests and people should be strengthened in their determination to observe the Vigil in its integrity even in the face of resistance and apathy. In many urban areas it will be possible for a number of parishes and communities to join together to celebrate the Vigil. Where that is done only one Paschal Candle should be used for the Service of Light but at the conclusion of the Eucharist the candles of other communities can be lit from the principal candle and carried out by their clergy or other representatives in the procession from the altar.

Three preliminary points of a general nature need to be made before we discuss the structure of the service and examine each of its sections. First of all, we need to remind ourselves of a truth which has been the major theme of our study, that the Easter Vigil is still the celebration of the whole mystery of redemption in its unity and integrity. If the separate commemoration of the crucifixion on Good

Friday has meant that the Gospel reading at the Vigil is now the account of the Resurrection only and no longer the whole narrative of the Passion, Death and Resurrection, yet still – to cite only a few examples – the *Exsultet*, the readings from the Old Testament and the Letter to the Romans, the baptismal liturgy and the Proper Preface emphasize the fact that we are celebrating the Christian Passover, the *transitus* of God's people and of his Messiah. The Vigil is of crucial importance because it is both the climax of Holy Week and the inauguration of the Great Fifty Days of Easter – Pentecost; it is the hinge which connects and unites the two[76]. Since Christian theology and devotion have been so impoverished by the divorce between the Cross and the Resurrection, between Lent and Easter, we have to persevere in the difficult but rewarding task of restoring to its full influence in the life of the Church the one liturgical celebration which proclaims with the fullest and most uncompromising clarity the New Testament unity of Cross and Resurrection.

Secondly, it is useful perhaps at this point to reflect on the nature of the symbolism used in the Holy Week ceremonies and pre-eminently in the Easter Vigil. Theatrical realism is avoided – although much mediaeval elaboration (of the Palm Sunday procession, for example) tended in this direction. As we have already seen, the Holy Week liturgy is not a kind of drama designed to *impress* us; its first concern is always to *involve* us. It often succeeds in being both extremely dramatic and wonderfully impressive, but this is never the main consideration[77]. The symbolism of Holy Week makes sparing use of the directly representational and concentrates on certain fundamental biblical and sacramental archetypes and images – fire, light, water, oil, bread and wine. The liturgical symbol of the Resurrection is neither the popular and harmless 'Easter Garden' of modern fashion nor the Easter Sepulchre of the mediaeval English rites (in which a crucifix and host were 'buried' on Good Friday and from which they were 'resurrected' on Easter morning);[77a] rather it is the Paschal Candle whose symbolism is all the more powerful for being entirely non-representational. The Paschal Candle is, in the colourful phrase of Dom Lambert Beauduin, "no mere accessory to the Vigil, but rather its hero, its principal personality"[78].

Thirdly, we will have to accept with realism and honesty the fact that the easter Vigil will never be able to claim – and probably should not attempt to do so – the same kind of popularity as the Midnight Mass of Christmas. It will always baffle those whose Christian commitment is minimal, and its symbolism, which works so powerfully for those who can open themselves up to its rich and complex background, will remain opaque for those who are indifferent to or ignorant of that background. As Mgr Pézeril has explained:

> to expect of liturgical signs that they should speak to the first comer who sets his eyes on them is to forget that they derive their meaning from the mystery of salvation. The liturgy can only speak to those who, at least obscurely, have already received the Word[79].

What is more worrying – and must not be accepted with complacency – is the apparent indifference of many committed Christians to the Vigil. To those who associate the Resurrection of Christ with sunrise we need to point out that the New Testament is silent as the 'moment' of the Resurrection; what happened very early in the morning ("towards dawn" or "as the sun was rising" or "at the first sign of dawn" or "while it was still dark") was the discovery of the empty tomb. In the Easter Vigil we have to do not with a celebration that attempts to capture the 'moment' of the Resurrection but with a passing over with Christ from darkness to light, from death to life. It must become once again the normal way of celebrating Easter not just for an élite but for the whole body of committed Christians.

When we turn to consider the structure of the Easter Vigil we are faced with two radically different projects. That which is described here is the traditional one laid down in the Roman rite and envisaged as one of the two options in *LHWE*. This consists of:

   i)   The Service of Light;
   ii)  The Liturgy of the Word;

iii)  The Liturgy of Baptism;
iv)  The Liturgy of the Eucharist.

The preferred option in *LHWE*[80] is:

i)  'The Vigil' - a series of readings with psalms and prayers;
ii)  The Service of Light, leading into the Gloria, Collect, Epistle, Psalm, Gospel[81] and Sermon;
iii)  The Liturgy of Initiation;
iv)  The Liturgy of the Eucharist.

Although there is an historical element in this new project - in the shape of a tenth-century precedent from Jerusalem - pastoral and psychological considerations predominate. It is argued that the movement from darkness to light is more convincing if the Service of Light comes after the Old Testament readings and is made the point of transition from 'waiting' to 'celebrating'. Without in any way attempting to deny the strength of this argument, we believe that the traditional order has a force and coherence of its own and makes sense not only historically but also liturgically (the Service of Light being a form of entrance rite) and theologically (the traditional opening providing - literally - the light by which the Old Testament is to be read and understood).

Historically, the Service of Light or *Lucernarium* evolved naturally from the domestic custom of the Jews whereby the mother of the household brought in the lamp for the evening meal which ushered in Sabbaths and festivals and a blessing for God's gift of light was said over it. It is quite possible that our Lord himself pronounced this blessing at the Last Supper: "Blessed be thou, O Lord our God, King of all eternity, who didst create the lamps of fire"[82]. The ceremony was therefore taken over quite naturally into the Christian Church for use at a vigil service or at an *Agape* (a communal fellowship supper). Indeed *The Apostolic Tradition* of Hippolytus in the third century makes provision for a deacon to bring in the lamp for the meal and for the bishop to give thanks: "We give you thanks, Lord, through your Son Jesus Christ our Lord, through whom you have shone upon us and revealed to us the inextinguishable light . . ."[83] It is from this background and possibly from the same century that one of the oldest hymns in our hymn books, the Greek *Phos hilaron* (still in use at Vespers in the Byzantine rite and now an option in Evening Prayer in the *Alternative Service Book*), has come down to us:

> O gladsome light, O grace
> Of God the Father's face,
> The eternal splendour wearing;
> Celestial, holy, blest,
> Our Saviour Jesus Christ,
> Joyful in thine appearing.[84]

In our own day there has been something of a revival of the *Lucernarium* in both Anglican and Roman Catholic circles, notably in the provision for *An Order of Worship for the Evening* in the new American Prayer Book[85] and in the solemn celebration of Vigil Offices on the eves of Sundays and Solemnities in some monastic communities (for example, at the Abbey of Bec in Normandy). We can easily understand how in the unique context of the Easter Vigil the *Lucernarium* developed into the rich and powerful symbolism of the new fire (a pre-Christian ritual, which may have originated in Ireland, 'baptized' by the Church) and the new light and gave the Western liturgy its most eloquent and lyrical piece of prose and one of its most elegant melodies in the Paschal Proclamation or *Exsultet*. To the existence of the Paschal Candle and of the song of praise (*laus cerei*, literally "praise of the wax-light") both S.Augustine and S.Jerome testify in the fourth century, S.Jerome indulging in some only too characteristically caustic comments about deacons showing off![86]

The significance of the Paschal Candle and the ceremonies connected with it have been discussed in an earlier chapter[87]; at this point one further general comment must suffice. The theme of light is one that connects not only with the whole movement of Christ's redemptive work, but also with the activity of Creation; for the Resurrection inaugurates a new creation, and S.Paul, quoting Genesis, underlines the unity between the creative and redemptive activity of God: "It is God who said, 'Let light shine out of darkness', that has shone into our hearts to enlighten them with the knowledge of God's glory, the glory on the face of Christ." (2 Corinthians 4:6). The theme of light is also intensely eschatological, pointing us to the *parousia*: "See that you have your belts done up and your lamps lit. Be like people waiting for their master to return from the wedding feast, ready to open the door as soon as he comes and knocks. Blessed those servants whom the master finds awake when he comes." (Luke 12:35-37).

The second part of the Vigil, the *Liturgy of the Word*, comes immediately after the singing of the *Exsultet*. The high drama of the Service of Light gives way to the sober intensity of meditative reading and, as the faithful extinguish their candles, some may be tempted to feel a sense of anticlimax. Yet this is in fact the core of the Vigil, and it should be characterized by a sense of expectant waiting as the Lord opens to us the scriptures and our hearts burn within us. Recent reforms have cut down the number of obligatory Old Testament readings (there were twelve in the Missal of Pius V and four in the *Ordo* of Pius XII) and the most recent Roman reform has given greater unity to the rite by placing the Epistle and Gospel in this section so that the eucharistic liturgy now begins with the Intercessions. The new Roman rite provides seven Old Testament readings and *LHWE*. twelve, but neither requires that all of them need necessarily be read at any one celebration of the Vigil. The reading from Exodus 14 is under no circumstance to be omitted and *LHWE* considers that the reading from Genesis 1 should also never be omitted. Those tempted to cut down the readings to a minimum should ponder the reminder that this Liturgy of the Word constitutes "the oldest feature" (*LHWE* Introduction) and "the fundamental element" (Roman rite, rubric 21) of the Easter Vigil. It is vital therefore that this section of the Vigil be neither pruned to the bare minimum nor rushed through at maximum speed. *Celebrating Easter* explains that:

the restored order for the Vigil has seven Old Testament readings chosen from the Law and the Prophets, which are everywhere in use according to the most ancient tradition of East and West, and two readings from the New Testament, namely from the Apostle and from the Gospel. Thus the Church 'beginning with Moses and all the Prophets' explains Christ's paschal mystery. Consequently, wherever this is possible, all the readings should be read so that the character of the Easter Vigil, which demands that it should be somewhat prolonged, be respected at all costs.[88]

This is not the place to give a detailed commentary on each of the readings; it must suffice to make a few remarks of a general character. First of all, we need perhaps to remind ourselves of their dual orientation, not just a preparation of the faithful for the celebration of Easter but a final and immediate preparation of the *electi* for the Sacraments of Initiation. So, for example, the first lesson from Genesis which tells the story of Creation prepares us not only for the new creation of the Resurrection but also for new creation in Baptism, though of course the latter is implicit in the former. Secondly, we can profitably reflect on the particular structure of this Liturgy of the Word which not only enhances its teaching role but gives it the character of a dialogue between God and his people. Each reading is followed by a responsorial psalm, by an invitation to silent prayer and then by a Collect which "collects" and sums up this time of silent prayer and interprets the message of the Old Testament readings for the present needs of the Christian congregation. A brief introduction to each Old Testament reading, though not expressly ordered, will also be found helpful [89]. Thirdly, in the traditional order the Old Testament readings are read in and by the light of the Paschal Candle, in a darkened church, a powerful symbol of the truth that Scripture only reveals its full meaning in the presence of the Risen Christ.

A moment of drama comes after the last of the Old Testament readings; as 'Glory to God in the highest' is intoned the bells, silent since Maundy Thursday, ring out, the organ, similarly silent, joins in the jubilation, the church is illuminated and the altar candles are lit. Then after the Solemn Collect, which thanks God for brightening "this night with the radiance of the Risen Christ", and the Epistle, which since the most recent reform, is now the great passage from Romans 6 which proclaims the paschal character of Baptism, the *Alleluia* (absent from the liturgy since the beginning of Lent) triumphantly returns. As Pope John Paul II has reminded us, quoting a phrase tradition- ally ascribed to S.Augustine, "we are an Easter people and *Alleluia* is our song"[90]. *Alleluia* is repeated several times as the refrain to the responsorial psalm, verses from Psalm 118. This psalm, the last of the *Hallel* psalms so intimately connected with the celebration of the Jewish Passover, is the Easter psalm *par excellence* and, as *Celebrating Easter* reminds us, "is so often cited by the Apostles in their Easter preaching " [91] (cf. Acts 4:11-12; 1 Corinthians 3:11; Ephesians 2:20; 1 Peter 2:7-8). The Gospel reading is taken from a Synoptic narrative of the Resurrection (Matthew in Year A; Mark in Year B; Luke in Year C), with the Johannine account reserved for the Mass of Easter Day. As is mentioned above in our account of Good Friday, it is significant that in the time of S.Leo, as we have seen already, it was the whole Johannine narrative of the Passion and Resurrection which would have been read at this point in Rome. The sermon which follows should not be regarded as optional.

The third part of the Easter Vigil, the *Liturgy of Baptism*, can take three forms. The most reduced is for churches - for example, churches of religious communiti- es - where there is no font. Here water is blessed in a simpler formula and used to sprinkle the faithful after the Renewal of Baptismal Promises. It is the practice of some religious communities, notably that of Taizé, to have solemn professions at this point: religious profession is nothing other than a particular application of the baptismal covenant. The second form is for use in churches which have a font but where there are no candidates for Initiation; baptismal water is solemnly blessed for use during the

Easter Season and the faithful renew their baptismal promises. The third, fullest and normative form provides for the solemn blessing of baptismal water, baptism and, if possible, confirmation and then the renewal of baptismal vows by all the faithful. It is on this normative form that we shall briefly comment, first of all by emphasizing how important it is to try and find candidates for initiation during this liturgy, for their own sake and for the sake of the faithful, with the proviso that they should be adults or the children of adults, who have been fully and properly prepared for this most solemn form of initiation[92].

The Litany of the Saints at one time occupied the faithful while the candidates for initiation and the clergy were out of sight in the baptistry; it can now accompany the procession of candidates, sponsors and clergy, led by the Paschal Candle, to the font. In places where the font cannot be seen by the people, water can be blessed and the candidates baptized in the sanctuary. Baptism enrols us as members of the People of God and fellow citizens with the saints in heaven; it is fitting therefore at this point that we should be made aware of our fellowship with the saints and of their continuing intercession for us[93]. The Prayer of Blessing over the baptismal water is a rich meditation on the theme of water as worked out in the Scriptures and repays careful study. It begins with Creation and works through Noah and the Exodus narrative to Christ's baptism in the Jordan, the flow of water and blood from his side upon the cross and his command: "Go out and teach all nations, baptizing them..." (cf. Matthew 28:19). In this rite the font is seen as the womb of Mother Church made pregnant by the risen Christ and the power of the Holy Spirit to bring forth children, and the Church is not afraid to make use of frankly sexual imagery when the Paschal Candle is plunged into the waters of the font[94].

The celebration of Baptism and Confirmation during the night of Easter is discussed in some detail in an earlier chapter[95] and we have already referred to the Renewal of Baptismal Vows[96], but at this point it is appropriate to return to this rite since it does represent, as we have seen, the culminating point to which our whole observance of

Lent has been guiding and directing us. The people stand with lighted candles and the principal celebrant stands before the great glowing pillar of the Paschal Candle and addresses them. He reminds them that through the paschal mystery they have been buried with Christ in baptism so that they may rise with him to a new life within the family of his Church. Now that the observance of Lent has been completed he invites them to join him in renewing their baptismal vows, their rejection of evil and their allegiance to Christ. In the alternative form provided by *LHWE* among its Supplementary Texts (pp 288 - 290) can be found the form of re-affirmation of our baptismal faith which was first worked out for the great service in Canterbury Cathedral on the Eve of Pentecost 1982 in the presence of Pope John Paul II: this is to be commended to Anglicans not only because of its ecumenical significance but also because it allows the Apostles' Creed to fulfil once more its original role as a baptismal creed, from which it was banished by the *Alternative Service Book.* After the prayer which concludes this renewal the people are sprinkled with baptismal water while the anthem *Vidi aquam* or a hymn is sung[97]. As two Anglican commentators have remarked: "Many who would not normally advocate the sprinkling of holy water might see in this particular action a powerful symbolism."[98].

The fourth, final and climactic element in the Easter Vigil is the Liturgy of the Eucharist, introduced by the Intercessions and in the Anglican rite by the Peace. *LHWE* provides a special Easter form for the Peace and suggests that the faithful exchange the Easter greeting familiar to Orthodox Christians, "The Lord (or, strictly, Christ) is risen! He is risen indeed!" Every celebration of the Eucharist is a paschal celebration, a celebration of the whole mystery of redemption in its inclusive unity, and a fervent and expectant anticipation of the End[99]. These characteristics however, are nowhere expressed and realized with such clarity and force as in this one celebration during the night of Easter, in this Eucharist which sums up the work of the Cross and the Sepulchre and celebrates them in the joy and the light of the Resurrection; seen here not as an

eleventh hour reversal of the defeat on Good Friday but as
the confirmation of a victory already won, as the seal and
sign of the Father's acceptance and approval of the self-
offering of Christ in his Passion. Recent liturgical reform in
the Roman and Anglican Communions has led to the
introduction into the Eucharistic Prayer of acclamations
borrowed from the Syrian rites which stress the eschatological character of the Eucharistic celebration:

> Christ has died:
> Christ is risen:
> Christ will come again.[100]

At this point it is important to recall the dominant and
controlling note of the Jewish Passover, the note of
expectation, the eager looking forward to the coming
definitive liberation, of which the experience of the Exodus
is the prototype and guarantee. J.Jeremias has written:

> That the Messiah would come on the night of the
> passover was both a Jewish and a Christian hope. Each
> year, therefore, during the passover night the primitive
> community awaited until midnight, in prayer and
> fasting, the return of the Lord. They prolonged the
> waiting into the hours after midnight. If he had not
> come bodily by cock-crow, then they united themselves
> with him in the celebration of table fellowship.[101]

Later in the same book Jeremias quotes S.Jerome's *Commentary on Matthew* (Chapter 25: The parable of the wise
and foolish virgins):

> It is a tradition of the Jews that the Messiah will come
> at midnight according to the manner of the time in
> Egypt when the Passover was (first) celebrated.
> Whence I think also the apostolic tradition has
> persisted that on the day of the paschal vigils it is not
> permitted to dismiss before midnight the people who
> are expecting the advent of Christ.[102]

The Paschal Eucharist is 'realized eschatology' *par excellence*; although it is at one level an acknowledgement that

the End still lies in the future, it is at another level (the sacramental level) the bringing into the present of the reality and power of that anticipated fulness.So, in speaking of the hope of Christ's Coming, Bishop Bell of Chichester could write; "What we hope for is the fulness of what we already possess in him. What we possess has its meaning only in the hope of his Coming."[103] The Paschal Eucharist makes real for us the past, present and future dimensions of Christ's paschal mystery, and the Night of Easter is sadly frustrated and unfulfilled if it does not lead into that climax. In the words of Melito of Sardis, which recall words said today over the Paschal Candle at the beginning of the Vigil:

> He is the Alpha and the Omega;
> He is beginning and end,
> beginning inexpressible and end incomprehensible.[104]

In trying to summarize the message of this most holy night it is difficult to improve on S.Augustine. We cannot do better than conclude with an excerpt from one of his sermons on the Easter Vigil:

> Our Lord Jesus Christ, having made this day a day of mourning by his death, changed it into a day of rejoicing by his resurrection. Now that we are solemnly commemorating both of these events, let us keep watch in memory of his death, and joyfully welcome his approaching resurrection. This is our annual festival, our Paschal feast, not, as prefigured for the people of the Old Law by the slaughter of a beast, but as fulfilled for the people of the New Law by the sacrifice of our Saviour. 'For Christ our Pasch is sacrificed.' ... In watching and praying we pass this night in which our Lord arose from the dead, the night that brought us the life where there is neither death nor sleep ... Life began for us in his risen body.[105]

## EASTER DAY

There is a certain tension in the celebration of the Easter Day Eucharist which is probably inevitable. On the one hand there will be a proper desire to emphasize the overwhelmingly greater importance which should be accorded to the Mass of the Easter Vigil – to the point perhaps of wondering whether at least in some communities it is really necessary to have a second celebration, whether one cannot emulate the practice of the primitive Church and the continuing rule of the Orthodox Churches in having only one Eucharist. On the other hand there will be the realization that in the hard reality of pastoral practice there will be more people present in most churches at the eucharistic celebrations of Easter Day then at the Vigil. While it is legitimate to see the Easter Vigil as the one great celebration of the whole Paschal Mystery and the Easter Day celebration as concentrating principally on the event of the Resurrection, it is of enormous importance that the whole of the Paschal Mystery should be celebrated at the Easter Day eucharists, particularly bearing in mind the needs of those members who will not have been in church for the Vigil or perhaps for any of the ceremonies of the *Triduum*. This consideration will particularly affect the choice of hymns and readings; preachers too will be well advised to draw on such material as the Proper Preface for Easter and to explain the significance of the Paschal Candle.

Already, in the fourth century, Egeria describes how at Jerusalem after the Easter Vigil in the Great Church "they at once go with singing to the Anastasis, where the Resurrection Gospel is read, and once more the bishop makes the offering"[106]. This second Easter Mass was certainly known in North Africa in the time of S.Augustine and he himself often preached both at the Vigil and at the second Mass. There is evidence for it from other parts of Christendom, but, typically, it did not take root at Rome until later; the first Roman texts of prayers and readings date from the seventh century.

The principal Eucharist on Easter Day should be celebrated with great joy and solemnity and provision should be made for the best-loved Easter hymns to be sung. The Easter Day Mass is one of the two Masses in the Roman missal in which the *Sequence* before the Alleluia chant remains obligatory (the other is Pentecost). The words and traditional plainchant for this dramatic hymn, *Victimae paschali* attributed to the eleventh-century Wipo of Burgundy, may be found at *NEH* 519, and although no provision is made for it in *LHWE* its use is to be commended to Anglicans. Together with the Easter *Quem quaeritis* trope – another example of the mediaeval tendency to amplify the proper of the Mass with free poetic compositions – this beautiful sequence, with its few sentences of dialogue, has been seen by some scholars as the origin of liturgical drama and the beginning of Western theatre[107]. Other particular features in the Roman rite include the possibility of using water blessed at the Vigil for the Sprinkling with Holy Water which can replace the penitential rite at the beginning of the Mass and during which the anthem *Vidi Aquam* is sung; the repetition of the renewal of baptismal promises which may replace the Nicene Creed and at the end of which the people may be sprinkled (unless this has happened at the beginning of Mass); and a formula of Solemn Blessing which may be used at the Vigil and on Easter Day. The inevitable tension felt by those planning today's worship is particularly apparent when it comes to deciding whether to repeat the Renewal of Baptismal Vows which is so integral a part of the Liturgy of Baptism at the Vigil at the masses of Easter Day; liturgical and pastoral considerations may pull in opposite directions. While *LHWE* contains advice on the observance of the Easter Season, it makes no special provision for Easter Day itself other than allowing that certain features which properly belong to Easter Night may be transferred *faute de mieux* to the Day.

There was a time when for Anglicans Evensong was extremely popular; for a variety of reasons (from fear of mugging to the lure of television) this is no longer the case. Yet with Evening Prayer on Easter Sunday the Paschal *Triduum* comes to a close and, where there is any chance of assembling a congregation, every effort should be made to give it a particular and festive character[108]. Evidence from the seventh century suggests that at least by that time Vespers on Easter Day had acquired a very particular character in Rome, though for a more detailed description we have to wait for the eighth-century *Ordo Romanus XXVII*. The newly-baptized were invited together with the faithful to the Lateran Basilica (at that time as a general rule only Cathedrals had baptistries), and the whole congregation went in procession first to the Baptistry and then to the Chapel of the Cross where confirmation had been conferred. This 'glorious office' (*gloriosum officium*) later spread to the rest of Western Christendom and seems to have had a more tenacious hold in parts of France and Germany than in Rome itself. A procession to the font seems to have been a particular feature of the liturgical life of the greater French churches in the seventeenth and eighteenth centuries. In his *Voyages Liturgiques de France* the Sieur de Moléon writes with particular enthusiasm of the procession *ad Fontes* in Rouen Cathedral, during which the holy oils and the paschal candle are carried to the font. "*Cette procession,*" he comments, "*est fort propre à faire souvenir les Chrétiens des voeux de leur baptême.*" Earlier in the same work he writes of a similar procession at Vespers (but this time on Easter Monday and directly after the Magnificat) in the church attached to the Hôpital de la Salpêtrière in Paris; the little girls of the institution are led in procession to the font and there one of them pronounces in a loud voice the renewal of baptismal promises. De Moléon expresses the wish that such a ceremony could take place in parish churches; one cannot help wondering whether this is one of the sources from which those who revised the Easter Vigil liturgy under Pius XII drew their inspiration[109]. In a later phase of the Tractarian Movement in the Church of England there was an attempt to revive this tradition and from its first edition in 1906 *The English Hymnal* provided for a procession at the end of Evensong with the singing of *O filii et filiae*[110], followed by a versicle and response and the Collect for Easter Even to be recited at the font. Provision for the Renewal of Baptismal Promises at Evening Prayer or at any other service on Easter Day is made in *LHWE*. However the evening office is treated, it should not be allowed to be an anticlimax; the joy which has characterized the celebration of Easter should be maintained.

# Notes

1. *LHWE*, Introduction, pp.1-2.
2. *Celebrating Holy Week* by David Austerberry (Mowbray, London, 1982) and two publications from Grove Books (Bramcote, Notts); No 41, *Keeping Holy Week* by Peter Akehurst (1976) and No 93, *Celebrating Lent, Holy Week and Easter*, by Trevor Lloyd (1985) are recent Anglican publications from moderate and evangelical backgrounds respectively. The work of the Joint Liturgical Group, *Holy Week Services* (SPCK, London, 1971 and 1983) shows that this interest is shared in the Free Churches and the Church of Scotland. The essay by the distinguished Methodist scholar, Gordon Wakefield, in the 1983 edition is particularly valuable.
3. *Art und Sinn der ältesten christlichen Osterfeier in Jahrbuch für Liturgiewissenschaft*, Band 14 (1934).
4. Hermann Schmidt, SJ, Hebdomada Sancta, 2 Vols (Herder, Rome, 1956–57), the first words of the Introduction.
5. See above, p.6.
6. Gregory Dix, *The Shape of the Liturgy*, (Dacre Press, London, 1945), Chapter XI.
7. Talley, op.cit., pp.39 and 232.
8. Josef A.Jungmann, SJ, *The Early Liturgy*, trans. F.A.Brunner, (DLT, London, 1960), p.261.
9. *Egeria's Travels to the Holy Land*, ed. John Wilkinson, op.cit. The account of Holy Week is to be found between pp.132 and 139.
10. cf. Talley, op.cit. p.51: "Distressing as Egeria's omission of detail can often be, here her failure to find anything more noteworthy about the paschal vigil is precious information indeed. Such omission means that the Jerusalem practice concerning which we have such rich information was, for all practical purposes, just what was considered normal in her home country."
11. The Church of the Resurrection, built by Constantine over the Tomb of Christ. See illustration on p.84.
12. See above, p.9.
13. *PL* 54.398A.
14. The Holy Week Liturgy of the ecumenical community of Taizé in France has had a considerable influence on the Reformed Churches of Europe. See also *From Ashes to Fire*, (Supplemental Worship Resources 8 of the United Methodist Church in America, Abingdon, Nashville, 1979); the work of the Joint Liturgical Group in this country has already been mentioned.
15. According to Egeria the fourth-century Church in Jerusalem celebrated this event on this day at the *Lazarium*, the church of Lazarus at Bethany.
16. Although the Eastern Church used to hold a procession on Palm Sunday – there is evidence that it existed in the eleventh century in Constantinople – it has fallen into disuse. See *The Lenten Triodion*, ed Kallistos Ware and Mother Mary (Faber and Faber, London, 1978) p.58.
17. *The Lenten Triodion*, op.cit. p.60.
18. *The Resurrection in liturgical life in the Orthodox Church*, in '*If Christ be not risen . . .*', (S.Mary's Annual for 1986, S.Mary's Bourne Street London), pp.36f. We are indebted to this essay, to the booklet *Christ – the New Passover*, by Valentine Zander (London, 1980, but originally

published in Russian in Paris in 1940), and to Archimandrite (now Bishop) Kallistos Ware's introduction to *The Lenten Triodion* (op.cit.) for the work in this section. It is from the *Trodion* that most of the liturgical texts quoted are taken. We are grateful also to Canon Hugh Wybrew, whose helpful comments have enabled us to make certain corrections in this 1994 edition.

19. J.D.Crichton, *Christian Celebration*, (Chapman, London, 1981), Part I, The Mass, p.108f.
20. J.W.Tyrer, *Historical Survey of Holy Week*, (Alcuin Club Collections XXIX, 1932), p.74. J.D.Crichton, *The Liturgy of Holy Week*, (Goodliffe Neale, 1971), p.11.
21. See above, Chapter V, note 1.
22. *LHWE* pp.73 and 75.
23. *S.Luke's Daily Missal*, (Dublin, 1975) Palm Sunday, para 5, p.123.
24. A.Nocent O.S.B., *The Liturgical Year*, (Liturgical Press, Collegeville, 1977), Vol.II, p.201.
25. Similarly, the 1979 American Prayer Book, again like the Roman Rite, provides a proper collect for every day in the Easter Octave.
26. See above, pp.10 and 11.
27. J.W.Tyrer, op.cit. p.80.
28. See above, p.11.
29. cf. Congregation for Divine Worship; *Celebrating Easter*, (Do 580), circular letter concerning the preparation and celebration of the Easter Feasts, (CTS, 1988), para 37.
30. An ancient Latin hymn for the procession with the oils, translated by Bishop Richard Rutt, has found favour with many Anglican Dioceses and a place in the *NEH*, 512.
31. *General Norms for the Liturgical Year and the Calendar* (1969), paras 18 & 19.
32. op.cit. p.179.
32a. There is indeed even an Old Testament background, especially in Hosea 6:1 & 2. The language here indicates a short interval rather than precise timing and allusion may be being made to pagan fertility cults of dying and rising divinities.
33. *Epist.*23, 12–13. (*PL* 16:1030).
34. *Epist.*55, 24. (*PL* 33:215)
35. See the Latin text of *The Constitution on the Sacred Liturgy*, para 88. This is difficult to translate literally into English; the official French translation gives "*la vérité du temps*".
36. op.cit. *Ministry & Ordination II*, 13, p.35.
37. cf. H.Thurston SJ, *Lent and Holy Week*, (Longmans, London, 1904), p.286.
38. For a study of this theme in great theological and spiritual depth, cf. W.H.Vanstone, *The Stature of Waiting*, (DLT, London, 1982).
39. *The Lenten Triodion*, op.cit. We are indebted for this reference to M.Perham and K.Stevenson, *Waiting for the Risen Christ*, A commentary on *LHWE* (SPCK, London, 1986), p.54.
40. cf. above, Chapter II, note 19.
41. Footwashing was at one time associated with the baptismal liturgy in parts of Western Christendom, either during the rites of initiation at the Easter Vigil as in Milan in the time of S.Ambrose or on this day as in parts of N.Africa in the time of S.Augustine, essentially as a preparatory rite for

those about to be baptized but open to others also.

42. *The Royal Maundy*: Archbishop Cranmer's criterion for retaining ceremonies was that they should be 'neither dark nor dumb' (*Of Ceremonies*, in the introductory material in the Book of Common Prayer). It has regretfully to be conceded that the Royal Maundy as practised in our own days (moving, splendid and memorable though it undoubtedly is) has become as dark and dumb as any of the ceremonies of the so-called 'Unreformed Churches'. The climax of the whole rite, the washing of the feet by the Sovereign, has been omitted. Surprisingly, William III was perhaps the last monarch to have performed it in person; it died out finally in the Hanoverian period, although as late as 1731 the Archbishop of York, as Lord High Almoner, washed the feet of the poor in the Chapel Royal on behalf of the King. (See Peter Wright, *The Pictorial History of the Royal Maundy*, Pitkin, London, 1981.) Yet, in spite of this omission, many secondary features, such as the wearing of girded towels and the carrying of nosegays as a protection against the smell of unwashed feet, have been retained which can only make sense if the footwashing is performed. The real danger is that the sign of 'personal service' performed by the Sovereign can now be interpreted more as an act of generosity – the distribution of purses – than as an act of real, Christ-like humility. A revival of the original Royal Maundy would be a powerful sign of the radical reinterpretation of the meaning of authority in the Christian tradition.

43. *Serm.*27,2. *PL.*38:1247.

44. op.cit.: Introduction, 5.

45. *The Rule of S.Benedict*, op.cit. cap LIII, pp.257–259.

46. cf. Perham and Stevenson, op.cit., p.61.

47. The *New English Bible* version is that printed in *LHWE*. The *New Jerusalem Bible* renders this as "without recognising the body"; a note adds: "This verse is most naturally taken as referring to failures to recognize Christ's presence and activity in the Eucharist (cf. v.27). However, the emphasis in this letter on the Church as the Body of Christ suggests that there may also be a reference to selfish individuals who ignore needy fellow-members of the Christian family (cf. vv.11 & 33)".

48. C.S.Lewis, *The Weight of Glory*, in *They Asked for a Paper*, (Bles, London, 1962), p.211.

49. Sermon, 'Our Present Duty', *Report of the Anglo-Catholic Congress, London, July 1923*, (SSPP, London, 1923) p.186.

50. J.T.Martin, *Christ our Passover*, (SCM, London, 1958), pp.29–30.

51. 'Of the glorious body telling . . .' *NEH* 268.

52. *Celebrating Easter*, op.cit. paras 55 and 56, pp.15–16.

53. cf. Thurston, *Lent and Holy Week*, op.cit. chapter IX.

54. Various experiments have been tried in Anglican churches to produce a 'Liturgical Three Hours' in which some or all of the liturgical services are interspersed with addresses and times for silent meditation. cf. eg *The Chichester Customary*. Today it is found effective in some churches to have a non-liturgical series of addresses, meditations and hymns of an hour and a half or two hours' duration, immediately preceding the Liturgy, timed to end at 3pm.

55. For the anticipation of the Easter Vigil in the Byzantine Rite today, see above p.91.

## Chapter VII

# The Great Fifty Days

aster Day is a climax; it is not a conclusion. By the middle
f the fourth century, as we have seen, the *Pascha* was
asically an all-night vigil from Saturday to Sunday, prepared
r originally by one or two days of strict fasting but now by
e forty days of Lent. But the *Pascha* had also its prolonga-
on – the great fifty days. These fifty days were viewed as
single and undivided whole, what Tertullian called "the
ost joyful period", *laetissimum spatium*; even as a single
y, what S.Athanasius called "the great Sunday", *magna
minica*[1]. During this time *alleluia*, forbidden in Lent, was
ng repeatedly and both kneeling for prayer and fasting were
ictly prohibited; a prohibition already recorded at the end
the second century and reiterated in the 20th canon of
caea in 325[2]. The only primitive distinction within that
riod was the special character given to the Easter Octave
elf, a feature taken over from the Jewish Passover (Exodus
:15–20 and Deuteronomy 16:1–8). In the Jerusalem of
eria's time there was a daily Eucharist during this week
gely because for those who had been baptized at Easter the
ek was a time for mystagogic catechesis – instruction on
e meaning of the Sacraments which, according to the
ciplina arcani of the early Church, had to be kept secret
n from the catechumens.[3] The newly-baptized continued
wear their white garments until the following Sunday –
own mysteriously until recent times as *dominica in albis
positis*), signifying the Sunday on which white robes were
l aside. Moreover, not only was there no Ascension Day

56. *Ep. xxv*.4. cf. J.W.Tyrer, *Historical Survey*, op.cit. p.119.
57. At one time, however, the Liturgy of the Presanctified was celebrated on Holy Friday in the Byzantine tradition. There is evidence of its use at Constantinople in the mid-eleventh century, but the practice had died out by 1200. See *The Lenten Triodion*, op.cit. p.62.
58. The revised *Ambrosian Missal* provides a rite which begins with the Liturgy of the Word, continues with the Veneration of the Cross and ends with the Solemn Prayers and a Blessing.
59. cf. J.G.Bishop, 'The Anglican Tradition' in *A Manual for Holy Week*, ed. C.P.M.Jones, (SPCK, London, 1967), pp.43–54.
60. J-B.Thibaut, *Ordre des Offices de la Semaine Sainte à Jérusalem du IVe au Xe siècle*, (Paris, 1926).
61. Louis Bouyer, *The Paschal Mystery*, op.cit., p.161.
62. cf. Dix, op.cit. p.440.
63. A.M.Ramsey, *The Narratives of the Passion*, op.cit. p.24.
64. cf. Maxwell E. Johnson, 'The Paschal Mystery: Reflections from a Lutheran Viewpoint' in *Worship*, Vol 57 no.2, March 1983.
65. G.Aulén, *The Faith of the Christian Church*, (Fortress Press, Philadelphia, 1960), pp 217–218.
66. *ASB*, Third Eucharistic Prayer of Rite A; cf. Eucharistic Prayer II of the Roman Missal. The phrase is taken directly from *The Apostolic Tradition* of Hippolytus.
67. *LHWE* argues that it is "much more logical and effective for the Proclamation of the Cross, where it is used, to follow the Passion Narrative" and therefore encourages the reversal of the traditional order of Solemn Prayers and Veneration. We would only ourselves encourage this reversal where there is no Communion, as in the Ambrosian Rite, cf. Note 58.
68. *NEH* 517.
69. J.A.W.Bennett, *Poetry of the Passion*, (Clarendon, Oxford, 1982), p.29. The dust jacket of this fascinating book reproduces an inscription by David Jones which incorporates a stanza of *Vexilla Regis* with a line from the Dream of the Rood and *Hagios Ischyros* from the Reproaches.
70. *Pange lingua*, *NEH* 517, v.7.
71. op.cit. p.223.
72. The cosmic significance of Christ's death and resurrection is far better illustrated in the Eastern iconographic tradition. cf. J.Baggley, *Doors of Perception*, (Mowbray, 1987), plates 15 and 18(ii) and text pp.41–42 and 148. cf. also Frontispiece.
73. It is possible that Herbert visited Venice. Certainly his friend Nicholas Ferrar did.
74. *Serm* 219; cf. P.T.Weller, *Selected Easter Sermons of S.Augustine* (Herder, S.Louis Missouri, 1959), pp.79–81.
75. op.cit. para.78.
76. The text of the Easter Vigil as first reformed in 1951 was given the title *Ordo Sabbati Sancti*, but in the present Roman Rite it is made quite clear that the Vigil does not belong to Holy Saturday but rather to Easter Sunday (*Dominica Paschae in Resurrectione Domini*) and in *LHWE* it is *the* Easter Liturgy *par exellence*.
77. If liturgy needs to shun theatricality, it is still close to theatre which at its best is also concerned with communicating "the invisible-made-visible"; cf. Peter Brook, *The Empty Space* (McGibbon and Kee, 1968; Penguin Books,

1972), chapter 2 – The Holy Theatre, passim.

77a. For a full discussion of the mediaeval English practice see Eamon Duffy: *The Stripping of the Altars* (Yale University Press, London, 1992) pp.29–37.

78. 'Le Cierge Pascal', in *La Maison-Dieu*, No 26 (1951).

79. Daniel Pézeril, 'Le mystère pascal et l'homme d'aujourd'hui', in *La Maison-Dieu*, No 68 (1961).

80. This option goes back at least to the first version of *Holy Week Services* by the Joint Liturgical Group (SPCK and Epworth, 1971). It was also adopted in an English Roman Catholic publication, *Lord, by your Cross and Resurrection: Celebrating Holy Week*, produced by The S.Thomas More Centre for Pastoral Liturgy in 1979.

81. The rubrics (23, note 6) permit the anomaly of no Gospel reading at this point if it has already been read at the 'Vigil'.

82. cf. *Louis Bouyer, Life and Liturgy*, (Sheed and Ward, London, 1956), p.129.

83. cf. *Hippolytus: A Text for Students*, ed. G.J.Cuming, (Grove Books, Bramcote, 1976), p.23.

84. *NEH* 247. John Keble's translation, "Hail gladdening light" is used in other hymn books eg *A&M New Standard* 8. Yet another version, "O Light Serene," is provided in the Roman Office for First Vespers of Sunday in the first and third weeks of the four week psalter.

85. Anthems at the Candle Lighting are provided in *The Book of Occasional Services*, (Church Hymnal Corporation, New York, 1979), pp.8–14. In 1991 the Liturgical Commission of the Church of England produced a book of liturgical material covering the season from Advent to Candlemas entitled *The Promise of His Glory*, (London, 1991). This contains a whole chapter devoted to *The Service of Light*. In 1992 the Society of St Francis published a version of the Daily Office called *Celebrating Common Prayer*. In the Office book there is further rich provision for the Service of Light.

86. *PL* 30, 182–7. cf. J.N.D.Kelly, *Jerome*, (Duckworth, 1974), p.111. It was some time before the text became a fixed one, and even then there was some variation. In particular the *felix culpa* passage ("O happy fault, O necessary sin of Adam, which gained for us so great a Redeemer") caused great offence. S.Hugh of Cluny ordered it to be effaced in his missal and the words have been omitted or crossed out in many mediaeval texts. This passage is missed out in the *LHWE* version.

87. See above, Chapter III, pp.45–46.

88. op.cit. para. 85.

89. Admirable introductions can be found in *Celebrating the Easter Vigil*, ed. Burger and Hollerweger, (Pueblo, NY, 1983). The book was originally published in German as *Dies ist die Nacht*.

90. In an address to the people of Harlem (New York), 2nd October, 1979.

91. op.cit. para. 87.

92. In the Roman Catholic Church adult candidates for baptism will, in the absence of a bishop, be confirmed by the priest who baptized them. Since presbyteral confirmation is not allowed by the present discipline of the Church of England, adults who are to be baptized during the Easter Vigil should therefore, if possible, be taken to a celebration presided over by a
bishop. Otherwise we suggest that they be admitted to Holy as "ready and desirous to be confirmed" [Prayer Book Order ation]; to refuse them communion on this occasion would b The initiation of adult candidates in the Roman Catholic C fully provided for in *RCIA* and in the pastoral, catechetical material that accompanies it. See *The Rite of Christian Initia A Study Book*, (S.Thomas More Centre, London, 1988).

93. In Anglican congregations where there are some who will about the direct invocation of saints it may be better not to u however, the refrain "Join in our prayer", sometimes used in for us" because it fits the music better, may be found easie some Anglicans.

94. cf. Gilbert Cope, *Symbolism in the Bible and the Church*, ( 1959), p.102.

95. See above pp.54–55.

96. See above p.9.

97. *For the Vidi Aquam* see above Chapter IV, p.59. A suitab be *NEH* 114, 'Now is eternal life . . .'

98. Perham and Stevenson, op.cit. p.111.

99. The BEM text on the Eucharist has a very fine section on as Meal of the Kingdom', which emphasizes this eschatol

100. A more literal translation of the Syrian original was provic of *Common Worship* of the Church of South India (OU death, O Lord, we commemorate, thy resurrection we c second coming we await.' Other acclamations available t Roman Catholics stress the same note, particularly that o the Proper Preface of Easter: 'Dying you destroyed our d restored our life, Lord Jesus, come in glory.' Some will themselves to the 'Christ has died' acclamation, so as n acclamation to God the Son in the middle of the Eu addressed to God the Father.

101. Jeremias, *The Eucharistic Words of Jesus*, op.cit. p.123.

102. ibid. p.206.

103. G.K.A.Bell, *The Kingship of Christ*, (Penguin, London,

104. Melito of Sardis, op.cit. 105, p.61.

105. *Serm. Guelf. V*: cf. P.T.Weller, op.cit. pp.82–86.

106. *Egeria's Travels*, op.cit. p.139.

107. Although this hymn is available in Anglican hymnbo admitted that its difficult plainsong melody has discourag use. Its words however are important, cf. Chapter III, p

108. cf. *Celebrating Easter*, op.cit. para. 98.

109. De Moléon, *Voyages Liturgiques de France*, (Paris, 171 Gregg International, Hants, 1969), pp. 261, 325–327.

110. *EH* 626. See also *NEH* 527 which provides an alternati

(which only appeared towards the end of the fourth century); there was not even a clear distinction between the *Pascha* as the celebration of the Cross and Resurrection and Pentecost as the celebration of the Descent of the Spirit. The whole period was described either as the *Pascha* or more commonly as Pentecost. For if Pentecost means literally 'the fiftieth' and therefore describes the fiftieth day, it came to mean for the early Church more often the whole period of fifty days – as in the 20th canon of Nicaea forbidding kneeling for prayer "in the days of the Pentecost". There is a vestigial reminder of this in the Old Vulgate translation of Acts 2:1, *Cum complerentur dies Pentecostes*, that is to say a plural form, "when the days of the Pentecost were completed", rather than the singular form of the Greek.[4]

The introduction of a chronological sequence working *backwards* from the Night of Easter into the days of Holy Week brought, as we have seen, both loss and gain; the loss being a weakening of the unity of the Paschal Mystery, a weakening of the unity between Cross and Resurrection. In the same way the introduction of a chronological sequence working *forwards* from the Night of Easter also brought both loss and gain; the loss being again a weakening of the unity of the Paschal Mystery, a weakening of the unity between Resurrection, Ascension and the Descent of the Spirit. This unity was broken in the latter part of the fourth century with the introduction of the Feast of the Ascension on the fortieth day after Easter. Following the accounts in Luke's Gospel and the Fourth Gospel, the Ascension had originally been commemorated either on Easter Day itself – stressing the continuity with the Resurrection, or at Pentecost, the fiftieth day – perhaps stressing the link with the gift of the Spirit. Under the influence of the chronology of Acts 1:3 and the historicization brought about by increased devotion to the Holy Places the commemoration was transferred to the fortieth day and treated as a feast in its own right. This in turn led to the introduction of the usual preparatory fast and the unity of the *laetissimum spatium* was sundered. The integrity of the fifty days was further compromised with the introduction of an octave of

Pentecost, as if this feast were a quasi-autonomous celebration of the Holy Spirit.

For all these reasons, the liturgical reform which had been concentrated first of all on Lent and Holy Week, was focussed after Vatican II on the Great Fifty Days also. It was re-affirmed that "The fifty days from Easter Sunday to Pentecost are (to be) celebrated in joyful exultation as one feast day, or better as one 'great Sunday'."[5] As a result the unity of the whole period is now more clearly emphasized: Ascension Day is no longer allowed to be seen as if it were the end of Eastertide, for the Paschal Candle (formerly extinguished after the Gospel on Ascension Day) remains in the sanctuary until after Evening Prayer on the Day of Pentecost and the Sunday after Ascension Day is now called the 7th Sunday of Easter in the Roman Rite and, more half-heartedly, subtitled Easter 6 in the *Alternative Service Book*. In *LHWE* it is suggested that a Preface of the Resurrection be used at the Eucharist daily and that Easter hymns be sung until Ascension Day[6]. Both Rome and the Church of England have made changes in their eucharistic lectionaries to stress the unity of the Easter Season. The Roman rite gospel selections for the Sundays *of* Easter recount the appearances of the risen Christ until the third Sunday and, to avoid interrupting the narrative, the old observance of 'Good Shepherd Sunday', previously kept on that day, is transferred to the following Sunday. The gospels for the remaining Sundays of Easter are excerpts from the discourse and prayer of Christ after the Last Supper. The *ASB* gospels for the Sundays *after* Easter present in Year 1 the resurrection appearances leading up to the Ascension, and in Year 2 the great "I am" passages from the Fourth Gospel. The Roman rite has adopted the usage of referring to the Sundays of Easter in order to stress the unity of the Great Fifty Days; this reform has also been adopted in parts of the Anglican Communion, notably in the 1979 American Prayer Book. The *Alternative Service Book* has retained Sundays after Easter, and this can lead to some confusion; Low Sunday, for example, is for some the 2nd Sunday *of* Easter, for others the 1st Sunday *after* Easter.

The days of fasting and prayer called Rogation Days (Latin: *rogare* to ask), on the Monday, Tuesday and Wednesday before Ascension Day, used to strike an alien note, having been first marked by penitential litanies in Vienne in Gaul in the fifth century under circumstances of natural and other disaster. Over the years they had become days on which the Church asked for God's blessing on the fruits of the earth and on human labour; days which, freed from their previous penitential character, should not intrude upon the joyful celebration of Eastertide. In the Roman rite it is now left to local episcopal conferences to decide on what day or days around this time a votive mass for 'productive land' or 'the blessing of man's labour' should be celebrated. For the Church of England, *LHWE* has a note stressing that the Rogation Days should be seen as part of Eastertide and more or less suppressing what was once known as Rogation Sunday in favour of the Fifth Sunday after Easter.[7] In the same way recent reforms in both Roman and Anglican rites have abolished the obser-vance of the Vigil of Pentecost (understood as the day preceding the feast) as a day of fasting.

More importantly perhaps, both Roman and Anglican rites have now abolished the Octave of Pentecost. Unfortu-nately, the *ASB* has not been consistent or coherent in its reform. It has implicitly abolished the Octave and no longer provides propers, as in the Book of Common Prayer, for Monday and Tuesday in Whitsun Week, yet it provides no ferial collect for use between Pentecost and Trinity Sunday, has a series of readings for Morning and Evening Prayer during the week that focus on the gift of the Spirit and orders the Preface of Pentecost to be used at the eucharist "until Trinity Sunday". It presumably presupposes red rather than green to be the appropriate colour for the week. It is to be regretted that *LHWE*, while emphasizing that "Pentecost, the Jewish Feast of Weeks, or Harvest, falls on the fiftieth day after Passover/Easter and marks the *end* (our italics) of the season", did not feel able to produce proposals for the week after Pentecost[8].

Some have chosen to misinterpret this reform as a downgrading of Pentecost; it is important to realize that it is nothing of the kind. First of all, even in the Old Testament, as Thomas Talley remarks, "in contrast to Passover and the Feast of Tabernacles, both of which were observed over a week, Pentecost was kept on a single day, although pilgrims assembled for it not only from Judaea but from Galilee and other parts."[9] For the Jewish Feast of Weeks was itself seen not as a new beginning but as a completion, the solemn conclusion of a period of fifty days or seven weeks (a 'Week of Weeks') whose beginning was defined by Passover. So too for the Christian Church Pentecost is both the fiftieth day and the solemn conclusion of a period of fifty days. It both sums up the mystery celebrated throughout those fifty days and links the particular event which it commemorates with all that has gone before it. It casts its shadow not so much before it as behind it, and, in particular, if it has lost an octave (which it should never have had) it has gained a novena, for, as *LHWE* forcibly reminds us, the days after Ascension Day constitute a "season of preparation for Pentecost" and "a time of prayer for renewal by the Holy Spirit" during which "hymns which call for the gift of the Holy Spirit are appropriate"[10].

The union of joyful exultation in the glorification of Christ and eager yearning for the promised outpouring of the Holy Spirit has been admirably captured in the Magnificat antiphon for Vespers on Ascension Day in the Roman Office, *O Rex Gloriae*:

King of Glory, Lord Almighty,
today you have ascended victoriously above the
  heavens:
do not leave us orphans without a guide,
but send the one whom you promised,
the gift of the Father, the Spirit of Truth, alleluia.

It is recorded of the Venerable Bede that during the days leading up to his death on the eve of Ascension Day, 735, this was one of the antiphons he found the strength to sing, though, "when he reached the words 'do not leave us orphans,' he broke into tears and wept much."[11] Cranmer adapted this antiphon to form the Collect for the Sunday

after Ascension Day and, in a slightly modernized form, it is
retained for this Sunday and the days of the following week
in the *Alternative Service Book*. The Pentecostal character
of these days has led to growing support for observing this
novena as an alternative period of prayer for Christian
Unity to the week from 18th to 25th January.

This new understanding of the Great Fifty Days has been
given fine liturgical expression in the new Preface for
Pentecost in the Roman Missal:

> Today you sent the Holy Spirit
> on those marked out to be your children
> by sharing the life of your only Son,
> and so you brought the paschal mystery to its comple-
> tion.

This preface may indeed be new but it echoes a passage
from a sermon on the feast of Pentecost attributed to
S.Augustine: "See how the solemnity of the Pasch has
reached its conclusion without losing any of its splendour.
The Pasch is the beginning of grace, Pentecost is the
crown"[12].

For a renewed understanding of Pentecost it has been
necessary to go back to the pre-Nicene and Nicene Church.
But it is necessary to go back further still, for just as the
Christian *Pascha* cannot be understood unless its Old
Testament and Jewish background is given the most
serious attention, so the same is true of the Christian
Pentecost and the Feast of Weeks. For although the content
of the Christian Pentecost is in one sense completely
new – the Descent of the Holy Spirit, there yet remains a
certain relationship with the Jewish Feast of Weeks which
needs to be explored and understood.

One element in Passover was the agricultural feast of
*Azymes*, Unleavened Bread, which took place on the
following day. It marked the beginning of the barley harvest
and comprised an initial offering of the first-fruits, a sheaf
of barley, to Yahweh. The harvest itself lasted seven weeks
and the real harvest festival, when the cereal offerings were
solemnly presented to the Lord, took place at the end of
that period, at Pentecost – the Feast of Weeks – one of the

three great pilgrimage feasts of the people of Israel. It is not altogether implausible to find a connection here with Christian celebration. According to S.Paul, our Lord is "the first-fruits of all who have fallen asleep" (1 Corinthians 15:20) and the idea of a Pentecostal harvest is familiar to many of the Fathers. Take for example a passage from S.Irenaeus which is one of the readings for Pentecost Sunday in the Roman Office: "For the Spirit brought the scattered races together into a unity, and offered to the Father the first fruits of all the nations."[13]

But just as the Passover of the Jews was an agricultural festival (or more strictly the union of a pastoral festival and an agricultural festival) which had come to be identified with an event in the salvation history of Israel, so it was with Pentecost – though this identification came much later and is not made in the Old Testament. In later Judaism it came to be the memorial day of the giving of the Law on Mount Sinai and the establishment of the Mosaic Covenant. Not much attention has been paid to this in the later Christian liturgical tradition; an honourable exception is Keble's hymn from *The Christian Year*:

> When God of old came down from heaven,
>     In power and wrath he came;
> Before his feet the clouds were riven,
>     Half darkness and half flame.
>
> But when he came the second time.
>     He came in power and love;
> Softer than gale at morning prime
>     Hovered his holy Dove.
>
> The fires that rushed on Sinai down
>     In sudden torrents dread,
> Now gently light a glorious crown,
>     On every sainted head. [14]

The link between the exodus from Egypt and the the Law-giving on Mount Sinai was important for the Jews, for – as the twelfth-century Jewish philosopher Moses Maimonides was later to explain – "the latter was the aim and object of the exodus from Egypt"[15]. The link was important too for the Fathers, who point out that in the Old Testament the Law was given to Israel written "with the finger of God" and that in the New Testament "the finger of God" is declared to be none other than the Holy Spirit himself. With the Christian Pentecost the guidance of the Spirit replaces the guidance of the Law. We cannot be sure that S.Paul's own contrast between the written code of the Mosaic Law and the Spirit in 2 Corinthians 3:6 is made consciously in the light of this understanding of Pentecost, but this link was certainly made in Patristic preaching.

Two conclusions can be drawn from all this evidence. The first must be that just as for the Jews Passover leads to Pentecost – the first-fruits leading to the harvest, the giving of the Law being seen as the object and aim of the exodus – so it is for us. *Pascha* leads to Pentecost: Christ rose from the dead to be the first-fruits of a new humanity, and that humanity first found its identity, its unity, its inner dynamism and its mission in the Descent of the Spirit at Pentecost. Jesus is the second Moses, but whereas Moses liberated the Israelites from Egypt in order to seal a covenant with God on Mount Sinai by means of the Law, Jesus liberates his people from the tyranny of sin and death in order to seal the new covenant in the gift of his Spirit. The Paschal Mystery is indeed brought to completion on the Day of Pentecost.

The second conclusion is that Easter and Pentecost belong to each other inseparably and indivisibly. So, paradoxically, we discover that Easter is a feast of the Spirit and Pentecost is a feast of Christ. The Resurrection is itself an outpouring of the Holy Spirit by the Father upon the Son: Christ is raised by the Spirit, transformed by the Spirit and in his resurrection has become "a life-giving spirit" (1 Corinthians 15:45). Conversely, at Pentecost we celebrate the new means of Christ's presence with and to and for his people, and we celebrate the Church as the Body of Christ, but only and precisely because it is filled and vivified by his Spirit. Thanks to Easter we have something to celebrate, thanks to Pentecost we have the possibility of celebrating; for it is by the power of the Spirit that the gifts of bread and wine which we bring to the altar become the Body and Blood of the crucified and risen Christ.

The Liturgy of the Feast of Pentecost itself has been reformed in the light of this understanding. In the Book of Common Prayer it was called Whit-Sunday (though 'Pentecost' appears among the Tables and Rules), a name which referred to the custom of baptizing on this day and, more particularly, to the white robes of the newly-initiated[16]. In the *Alternative Service Book* it is called Pentecost (with Whit-Sunday in brackets) and additional readings are provided for the eucharistic liturgy, including the account from Exodus 19 of the giving of the Law on Mount Sinai. The 1979 American Prayer Book provides for an evening Vigil of Pentecost beginning with the Service of Light and including a baptismal liturgy on the model of the Easter Vigil. In the new Roman Missal the old vigil mass of Saturday morning with its six Old Testament prophecies and blessing of the font has been replaced by an evening vigil mass which is not explicitly baptismal but provides readings with strong baptismal allusions. The mass of the day gives prominence to a Gospel reading which must be used at least once every three years and may be used every year; the same reading is also one of two Gospel passages provided by the *Alternative Service Book*. The reading in question is the account from the Fourth Gospel (John 20:19-23) of the appearance of the Risen Christ to his disciples on the evening of the first Easter Day. It had no place in the former eucharistic lectionaries for this day in either Church.

The Johannine account of the gift of the Spirit on the first Easter Day is crucial for any understanding of the profoundly theological basis of the unity between Easter and Pentecost. This unity is already anticipated in the 7th chapter of John, in the passage appointed as the Gospel for the vigil mass of Pentecost in the new Roman lectionary and as the second lesson for Evening Prayer on the Eve of Pentecost in the *Alternative Service Book*.

Jesus stood and cried out: 'Let anyone who is thirsty come to me! Let anyone who believes in me come and drink! As scripture says, "From his heart shall flow streams of living water" He was speaking of the Spirit which those who believed in him were to receive; for there was no Spirit as yet because Jesus had not yet been glorified. (John 7:37-39)

The hour of Christ's glorification is the hour of the Cross and Resurrection. In the hour of his death he cries "It is finished" and he gives up - or, rather hands over - his Spirit, while blood and water gush from his side. And so it is on the first Easter Day, which is for the Fourth Gospel both *Pascha* and Pentecost, that the risen and glorified Christ, filled with the Spirit, and utterly transparent to the Spirit, breathes on his disciples and says to them "Receive the Holy Spirit." (John 20:22)[17].

## Notes

1. Tertullian, *De Baptismo* 19; Athanasius, *Epist.fest.* 1.
2. On the Day of Pentecost at Vespers the Byzantine Rite has a "kneeling office", both a solemn invocation of the Holy Spirit and a reminder that at the conclusion of the Great Fifty Days the ban on kneeling comes to an end.
3. Talley, op.cit. p.55. Wilkinson (*Egeria*), op.cit. p.39. S.Cyril's *Five Mystagogical Catecheses* are available in an edition by F.L.Cross (SPCK, London, 1951).
4. Many will be familiar with these words from Palestrina's great motet but, curiously, although both Old Vulgate and Breviary have *Cum*, Palestrina's motet begins *Dum complerentur...*
5. Sacred Congregation of Rites, *General Norms for the Liturgical Year and Calendar*, (Vatican Polyglot Press, 1969), chapter I, para. 22.
6. *LHWE*, op.cit. p.274.
7. Although the Sunday theme suggested in the *ASB* is "Going to the Father" and the lections are clearly geared to Eastertide, the collect retains a decidedly Rogationtide flavour.
8. It is to be hoped that the Church of England Liturgical Commission will now be able to turn its attention to suggesting suitable collects for use on the weekdays after the Feast of the Baptism of the Lord (Epiphany I), the Feast of Pentecost and Trinity Sunday; possibly existing collects for Sundays after Epiphany or Pentecost which are not observed in that particular year.
9. Talley, op.cit. p.59. cf Deuteronomy 16:1-15.
10. *LHWE* op.cit. p.276.
11. *Letter of Cuthbert*; cf Leo Shirley-Price's Introduction to the Penguin Classics edition of *A History of the English Church and People*, (Harmondsworth, 1955), p.9.
12. This attribution is made by John Gunstone, *The Feast of Pentecost*,

(Faith Press, London, 1967), p.49, following Dom E. Flicoteaux, *Le Rayonnement de la Pentecôte*, (Cerf, Paris, 1957). We have not been able to trace the quotation.

13. *Adversus Haereses*, Book III, 17:1-3.
14. *EH*, 158. Unfortunately this hymn does not appear in *NEH*, though it does appear in *Hymns Ancient and Modern New Standard*, 90.
15. *Doctor Perplexorum*, III, 43.
16. The opening rubric of the baptismal liturgy in the First English Prayer Book of 1549 recalls this tradition: "It appeareth by ancient writers that the Sacrament of Baptism in the old time was not commonly ministered but at two times in the year, at Easter and Whitsuntide, at which times it was only ministered in presence of all the congregation: which custom now being grown out of use, although it cannot for many considerations be well restored again, yet it is thought good to follow the same as near as conveniently may be ..."
17. Some of the material in this chapter first appeared in *Kairos* No.9., (Easter 1984) and owes much to Robert Cabié, *La Pentecôte*, (Desclée, Tournai, 1965).

# Chapter VIII

# The Rediscovery of Easter

In a sense of course Easter has never been lost or forgotten: it has always been a source of joy and confidence to Christians in every generation, and belief in the Resurrection has always and everywhere been at the very centre of Christian faith. Yet to talk of the 'rediscovery' of Easter in our time is not an unfair exaggeration. Certainly Easter has failed to touch the hearts and imaginations of Christian people in the West in the same way as Christmas. The popularity of Christmas is easily understandable: it can make some kind of appeal even to people whose Christian faith is minimal or non-existent, and it has collected to itself a wealth of folklore and tradition.

In Western Christendom since the Middle Ages, the Passion has made more of an impact than the Resurrection and has come to be seen in separation from it; this is true moreover for Roman Catholics, Anglicans and Protestants. One has only to think of the Stations of the Cross[1], of Bach's Passions and Chorales, of the typical western crucifix (or crucifixion scene in painting or stained glass), of such hymns as that by the great 18th-century Nonconformist, Isaac Watts, *When I survey the wondrous Cross* (The 'protestant crucifix in verse', as it has been called), and of the whole range of western devotional, musical and artistic expression of this theme to realize a distinct lack of balance. The reasons for this divorce are many and complex and have never been the object of adequate systematic investigation[2]. The Latin doctrine of the Atonement, articulated most fully by Anselm (d.1109) in his *Cur Deus homo?*, with

159

its emphasis on the satisfaction required by the Father of the Son, was elaborated but not fundamentally altered by the Scholastic theologians of the later Middle Ages. It was fully in harmony with the developed penitential system of the Western Church and shared its legalistic preoccupations. The fact that this view of the Atonement stressed the work which Christ performed as *man* in relation to God led inexorably to a deep and tender but unbalanced devotion to the sacred humanity of Christ and to his suffering and death, which was to be further developed in the spirituality of the Cistercians in the twelfth century and of the Franciscans in the thirteenth century[3].

After the Black Death had swept across Europe in the fourteenth century, decimating the population and leaving scarcely a single community untouched, Christian iconography and popular devotion became obsessed with the suffering and death it had witnessed. A profound sense of sin and penitence led to an increased emphasis on the cost of redemption and thus to an increasingly realistic portrayal of the human agony of the Saviour. Here popular piety effectively completed the process Scholastic theology had begun. The description of Christ's sufferings in the *Revelations* of S.Bridget of Sweden (d.1373) represents perhaps the most influential literary expression of this trend, the *Imitatio Christi* of Thomas à Kempis (d.1471) its best known devotional expression, while the Isenheim altarpiece of Matthias Grünewald (d.1528) is one of the most memorable works of art produced under the same impulse. Certainly the Passion can make more of an impact on our human sensibilities, because suffering and death are basic and common human experiences, whereas resurrection from the dead is manifestly not. But for the Christian the Passion is important because it is redemptive, and in the context of redemption we are now able once again to see that it is inseparable from the Resurrection.

The dangerous divorce of Cross and Resurrection is not only a matter affecting the liturgical, devotional and imaginative life of the Church; it has also had a baleful influence on the Church's theology. For the truth of the old maxim - *lex orandi, lex credendi* - operates in both directions. Liturgy can both express and influence theology; theology can both express and influence liturgy. This mutual influence has worked for better and for worse; it can be seen at work in the history of the divorce between Cross and Resurrection and it can be seen at work also in the history of the rediscovery of their unity. One of the pioneers of the rediscovery of this theological unity, the veteran French Redemptorist theologian, F.-X. Durrwell, wrote:

> Not so long ago theologians used to study the Redemption without mentioning the Resurrection at all. The fact of Easter was made to yield its utmost value as a piece of apologetics; but no one thought of examining it in itself as one of the inexhaustible mysteries of our salvation. Christ's work of redemption was seen as consisting in his incarnation, his life and his death on the cross. The theologians stressed the note of reparation, of satisfaction, of meritoriousness in that life and death, and generally they went no further. When the Resurrection was mentioned, it was not so much to give it any part in our salvation as to show it as Christ's personal triumph over his enemies, and a kind of glorious counterblast to the years of humiliation he had endured to redeem us. In short, Christ's resurrection was shorn of the tremendous significance seen in it by the first Christian teachers, and relegated to the background of the redemptive scheme. Such blindness naturally impoverished the whole theology of the Atonement.[4]

Durrwell's *magnum opus* was first published in 1950 and has had a considerable influence. However, in a footnote to the 11th French edition of 1982 the author acknowledges that his criticism retains some its validity even today and quotes a work published in 1972:

> Strange as it may seem, the resurrection of Christ, that is to say the central event in which is summed up the whole of Christianity, has not yet been made the object of very thorough reflection in the realm of dogmatic theology.[5]

A similar rediscovery to that of Durrwell had been pioneered within the Church of England by a remarkable pair of Cambridge theologians, Sir Edwin Hoskyns and Noel Davey, although their classic presentation of their theme *Crucifixion-Resurrection* was only published posthumously in 1981[6]. But already in 1945 the future Archbishop of Canterbury, Michael Ramsey, who had absorbed and made his own the teaching of his master Hoskyns, had written:

> It would be absurd to say that the West lost sight of the Resurrection, for every saintly life and every achievement of Christian thinking bears witness to it. Yet there have been phases in the West when the Cross was isolated and seen without the light of Easter upon it. The tendency can be traced in art, where the crucifix with the figure of the dead Christ upon it replaced the earlier 'Majestas' crucifix with Christ crowned, robed and victorious. It can be traced in doctrine, where the sacrifice of the atoning death has often been separated from the victory of the atoning Resurrection. It can be traced in worship, where the commemoration of Calvary in the liturgy has replaced the commemoration of the whole drama of God's redemption. In all this, sweeping generalizations are out of place. It is often inevitable for Christians to fix their gaze solely upon "Jesus Christ and him crucified," to know nothing save the Cross; and when they do they are indeed near to the Resurrection. None the less there has sometimes been a concentration upon the Cross that is less than Pauline, and there is a germ of truth in Westcott's words: 'It has been indeed disastrous for our whole view of the Gospel that a late age placed upon the Cross the figure of the dead Christ, and that we have retained it there.'[7]

The 'rediscovery' of Easter has been the fruit of a number of convergent movements of renewal in the Church. It has been due to the Biblical Theology movement of the 1940s and 1950s and the renewed attention paid to the basic *kerygma* (preaching) of the Apostolic Church. It has been due also to the renewed study of the Greek and Latin Fathers and a wider interest in and better understanding of their teaching. It has obviously been due in a very large measure indeed to the Liturgical Movement and to three aspects of it in particular; that concerned with historical research, that concerned with the articulation of a liturgical theology, and that concerned with a pastoral care for seeing that liturgy really communicates its message to the faithful. In this connection it is right to single out one particular name, that of Dom Odo Casel of the Benedictine Abbey of Maria-Laach, whose whole life was dedicated to the understanding and propagating of the theology of the Christian Mystery and its liturgical expression: he died with singular appropriateness on the night of Easter 1948 just after he had proclaimed as deacon the good news of the light of Christ – *Lumen Christi!*[8]

Another influence has been the Ecumenical Movement. Christian writers of all traditions have contributed to this rediscovery, and the restored Holy Week rites of the Roman Catholic Church have been adopted or adapted not only by Anglicans and Lutherans and the Community of Taizé, but more widely in the Reformed and Free Church traditions[9]. It is important to realize that this movement in the Western Churches has been due in some measure to renewed contact with the Orthodox Churches of the East, which have not suffered from the divorce introduced between the Cross and Resurrection in the West; indeed, they have kept and guarded the unity of the two in their theology, their liturgy and their devotion. As we have seen, their Holy Week liturgy has to some extent suffered from changes that obscure its full impact[10], but it has never ceased to be a potent and dominant influence in forming the faith and devotion of the Orthodox faithful. It has been a revelation to Western Christians to attend the great Easter midnight service and to feel the intense faith and jubilation of the Orthodox expressed in this magnificent rite. The Orthodox have become accustomed to living as a minority among Moslems or, until recently, under Communist rule; they have experience of suffering and persecution, and of situations in which the liturgy has been the sole teaching vehicle permitted to them. For them, as for the early Christians, the conviction of Christ's resurrection has been the sustaining and invigorating power in their life and witness. "Christ is risen! He is risen indeed!"[11]

Today Christians in the West are also having to accustom themselves to living as a minority in a world which, if not hostile, is certainly indifferent; we all need the heroic spirit of the early Christians, and to recover that spirit we need to feed on the paschal celebration of the Christian Mystery. This will require considerable effort, discipline and self-sacrifice. It is not easy for the clergy to build up a really corporate keeping of Holy Week in the parishes, nor for the laity to give up the time demanded. This is especially difficult nowadays when more and more people are away from home for Easter and when Maundy Thursday evening is the occasion for a mass exodus from our cities, so making a proper and recollected observance of the *Triduum* extremely difficult. We need increasingly to realize that the whole of Lent has been preparing us for these last few days and that nothing in the whole year is more important to our Christian life than the way we live through the Paschal Solemnity. The whole movement of renewal in the Church finds its concentrated essence in this restoration of the Easter Vigil and this new awareness of the Resurrection.

There are signs that this lesson is beginning to be assimilated. It has been helped by the continuing work of liturgical revision, so that most Churches which have any kind of liturgical tradition now have good liturgical material for Holy Week and Easter. It has been helped by the opening up of Christian imagination to the powerful symbolism of the Holy Week rites by artists and poets of the calibre of David Jones[12]. It has been helped too by the work of anthropologists and sociologists. As early as 1908, Arnold van Gennep isolated and named a category of ritual in all cultures called 'Rites of Passage'[13]. These are the transitional rituals which accompany changes of place, state, social position and age in a culture. The rites can be seen to have a basically three-fold, processual structure consisting of separation, liminality and reaggregation. The correspondence with Christian Initiation is immediately obvious but this insight also makes clear how deep-seated is the appeal behind such ideas as *Transitus*, Passover, Exodus and pilgrimage. In addition, the work of the psychologist C.G.Jung, who located the special power of symbols – including those used in the Paschal liturgy – in pre-conscious attitudes or even man's collective unconscious, and that of the theologian Paul Tillich, who related Jung's symbols to religious experience, has led to an increase in awareness amongst all Christians both of the continuing potency of the traditional paschal symbols and of the deep resonances they evoke even in those who at a conscious level would claim to have become impervious to the Christian message. There is also a growing understanding by Christians in the Evangelical tradition that the dismantling of the traditional ceremonies at the Reformation was due not only to Reformation theology but also to another very potent influence in the sixteenth century; the 'Gutenbergian revolution', brought about by the invention of printing during the fifteenth century, which led many people to become intoxicated with the power of words and to imagine that all teaching had to be communicated verbally and orally. In the twentieth century, the age of television and the 'hidden persuaders' of the advertising agencies, we have learned once more that words, spoken or printed, are not enough for communicating a message.

In the Roman Catholic Church the new *Rite of Christian Initiation of Adults*, and the revived catechumenate which goes with it, are a direct result of the 'rediscovery' of Easter and the Lenten journey of which Easter is the goal. As the introduction to the new rite puts it:

The whole initiation has a paschal character, since the initiation of Christians is the first sacramental sharing in the death and rising of Christ and since, moreover, the time of purification and enlightenment or illumination ordinarily takes place during Lent, with the postbaptismal catechesis or mystagogia during the Easter season. In this way Lent achieves its full force as a profound preparation of the elect and the Easter

Vigil is considered the proper time for the sacraments of initiation.[14]

But at the local level, in Roman Catholic parishes and those of the Church of England where the Adult Catechumenate movement has taken root, the process has worked in the reverse direction and interest in the Christian initiation of adults – perhaps inspired by a sense of the mission and outreach of the Church – has led to the rediscovery of Lent, Holy Week and Easter in all their richness.[15]

However, if there are indeed signs of hope in today's Church, there are also warning signs that all is not as well as we might want to believe. Parish priests, if they are honest, have often to confess to great discouragement in their efforts to encourage the faithful to take part in the Easter Vigil and to make the Vigil really come alive; some have allowed that discouragement to cause them to give up the struggle altogether.The comment of a very perceptive parish priest surely bears this out:

> It is the Easter Vigil congregation that is thin. And just a little mystified. In a sense, they are Calvary-Christians. For them, Good Friday is climax; Easter is epilogue. They do not see the event that altered the course of history as it really is; as death-resurrection. The hyphen is connection, follow-through. Holy Saturday was once an air-lock in the flow of Holy Week and the Vigil almost a secret ceremony . . .[16]

In 1988 the Vatican Congregation for Divine Worship issued a circular letter *Celebrating Easter* on the preparation for and celebration of the Easter Feasts. This letter faces up to the problems with honesty and realism, confessing that

> In some areas where initially the reform of the Easter Vigil was received enthusiastically, it would appear that with the passage of time this enthusiasm has begun to wane. The very concept of the Vigil has almost come to be forgotten in some places with the result that it is celebrated as if it were an evening Mass, in the same way and at the same time as the Mass

celebrated on Saturday evening in anticipation of the Sunday.

It also happens that the celebrations of the Triduum are not held at the correct times. This is because certain devotions and pious exercises are held at more convenient times and so the faithful participate in them rather than in the liturgical celebrations.

Without any doubt one of the principal reasons for this state of affairs is the inadequate formation given to the clergy and the faithful regarding the paschal mystery as the centre of the liturgical year and of the Christian life.

The holiday period which today in many places coincides with Holy Week and certain attitudes held by present day society together present difficulties for the faithful's participation in these celebrations.[17]

At the level of theological reflection too there are signs of a malaise, and in one of the most recent comprehensive studies of the Resurrection to be published, the distinguished Jesuit, Gerald O'Collins, Dean of the Faculty of Theology at the Gregorian University in Rome, can write:

Through being non-symbolic, non-experiential and non-liturgical, many recent Christologies have not appreciated and furthered the communication of the risen Christ. Often they have been especially good at using scriptural and historical scholarship. But to the extent that they have persistently refused to explore relevant symbols, reflect imaginatively on profound human experience, and draw on the Church's liturgy, they have failed to play their part in communicating successfully the presence of the risen Lord.[18]

And a little later he writes:

How many Western European, North American or Latin American theologians draw on liturgical sources and devotional practices to explore and present the saving 'work' and divine identity of Jesus Christ? And yet it is forms of worship, with the music and the visual art which accompany them, that primarily transmit to believers what they experience and know about the risen Lord. Liturgy is the great vehicle of tradition which evokes and hands on belief in him as living and present . . . The liturgy clearly supports starting with the paschal mystery and centering Christological thinking there . . . Thus any Christology which follows the witness of Christian worship will centre itself on the paschal mystery. That would enable it to communicate more effectively with believers who express and experience their faith primarily in terms of Christ's dying and rising.[19]

Perhaps therefore we still need a radical revolution in outlook and mentality before this centrality of the paschal mystery and of its liturgical celebration really takes hold of us. Such a revolution however must be brought to pass and the pascal mystery moved to the centre of consciousness of the whole Church and of every Christian.

## Notes

1.  It is only very recently that in many places a 15th Station has been added in honour of the Resurrection; see, for example, recent editions of the (Anglican) Walsingham Pilgrims' Manual.

2.  Nevertheless, see G.Aulén, *Christus Victor*, (trans. A.G.Hebert, SPCK, London, 1931), which provides a masterly survey of the historical material.

3.  See G.L.Prestige, *Fathers and Heretics*, Bampton Lectures for 1940, (SPCK, London, 1940), Lecture VIII. That, on the other hand, the full patristic theology of the Paschal Mystery and a doctrine of redemption that embraces both cross and resurrection were still very much living realities for the twelfth-century Cistercians has been demonstrated by Alf Härdelin in *Pâques et Rédemption* (Collectanea Cisterciensia, fasc. I, 1981).

4.  Durrwell, op.cit. Foreword, p.xxiii.

5.  C.Geffré, O.P., *Un nouvel age de la théologie*, (Paris, 1972) p.123.

6.  Hoskyns and Davey, *Crucifixion-Resurrection: The Pattern of the Theology and Ethics of the New Testament*, edited by Gordon Wakefield, (SPCK, London, 1981).

7.  A.M.Ramsey, *The Resurrection of Christ*, (1945), p.117. This citation is from Westcott's *The Revelation of the Risen Lord*.

8.  A judicious, critical but sympathetic appraisal of Casel's often controversial views can be found in Klauser, *A Short History of the Western Liturgy*, translated by John Halliburton, 2nd Ed (Oxford, 1979), pp.24–30.

9. For example, The Joint Liturgical Group, *Holy Week Services*, (SPCK, 1983) and the United Methodist Church of America, *From Ashes to Fire*, (Abingdon, 1979).
10. see above, Chapter VI, pp.91–92
11. cf. Timothy Ware, *The Orthodox Church*, (Penguin, 1963), pp.230–4 and 306–8.
12. David Jones, *In Parenthesis*, (Faber, 1937). See also T.Dilworth, *The Liturgical Parenthesis of David Jones*, (Golgonooza Press, Ipswich, 1979).
13. Arnold van Gennep, *The Rites of Passage*, (new edn., Routledge and Kegan Paul, 1960).
14. *Rite of Christian Initiation of Adults*, (Geoffrey Chapman, 1987), Introduction, para. 8.
15. For the Adult Catechumenate Movement in the Church of England see P.Ball, *Journey into Faith*, (SPCK, London, 19840; P.Ball, *Adult Believing*, (Mowbray, London, 1988), and for an Evangelical Anglican perspective on the new *RCIA*, P.Tudge, *Initiating Adults*, (Grove Books, Nottingham, 1988). Sadly, whilst advocating the traditional pattern of Lenten catechesis and Easter initiation, Canon Peter Ball fails completely to expound the profound theological link between the Paschal Mystery and the sacraments of initiation. On the other hand, J.D.Crichton in his contributions to *The Rite of Christian Initiation of Adults: A Study Book*, (S.Thomas More Centre, London, 1988), admirably elucidates the pascal theology of the new extended rite. A moving testimony to the success of *RCIA* in an American parish is given by a recent video production issued by Liturgical Training Publications in Chicago. The video is entitled *This is the Night*.
16. Peter Ignotus: *A Parish Diary* in *The Tablet* of 10.3.84.
17. op.cit. p.3.
18. Gerald O'Collins, S.J., *Jesus Risen*, (DLT, London, 1987), p.201.
19. ibid. p.203–4.

# Index

absolution, formula for; 100
acclamations; 92, 137
*Acts of Andrew*, apocryphal; 70
Adam; 11, 15, 49, 68ff, 125
*Ad cenam Agni providi*; 21, 58
Adult Catechumenate Movement;
  166
Advent Sunday; 96
*Agape*; 74, 130
*Alleluia*; 134, 139, 148
Altar of Repose; 81, 113, 123
*Alternative Service Book, 1980,
  The*; 2, 19, 54, 67, 80, 81, 99,
  102, 124, 125, 131, 136, 150,
  153, 156
Ambrose, S. 20, 104
Ambrosian Rite; 2, 116, 125,
  144n58, 145n67
American Prayer Book, 1979; 62,
  99, 120, 131, 150, 156
*anamnesis*; 41, 60
*Anastasis*, Church of the; 84, 86,
  87, 139
  Icon of; frontispiece, 125
Anicetus, Pope; 5
Antecommunion; 114, 116, 124,
  125.
Anselm, S. 159
antisemitism; 122
*Apostolic Tradition, The*; 7, 8, 130
Aquinas, Thomas, S. 113
*ARCIC*; 16n6, 33n16, 61, 65n20 &
  21, 106, 110
Ascension, Feast of the; 6, 149, 150,
  151, 152, 153
ashes, imposition of; 11, 12, 100
Ash Wednesday; 2, 10, 11, 12, 99,
  100
*Asperges*;65n16
Athanasius, S. 2, 148

atonement 49, 159-160, 162
Augustine, S. 57, 65n19, 76, 104,
  110, 126, 131, 134, 138, 139, 153
Aulén, Gustaf 120
*Azymes*; 29, 153


Bach, J.S. 159
Baptism; 3, 7, 12, 14, 22, 25, 47,
  53-57, 60, 127, 130
  Roman Rite of; 54
  Anglican Rites of; 54
  in Early Church; 54-55
*Baptism, Eucharist, Ministry.
  (BEM)*; 57, 65n9, n17 & n18; 146n99
Basil, S. Liturgy of; 90, 91
Beauduin, Dom Lambert; 82,
  129
Bec, Abbey of; 131
Bede, the Venerable; 18, 152
Bell, George, Bishop of Chichester;
  138
Benedict, S. (Rule of); 9, 110
Bernard of Clairvaux, S. 119
Blessed Sacrament; 113, 123
Boulding, Dame Maria; 32, 64,
  79n19
Bouyer, Louis; 16, 40, 41, 118
Bridget, S 160
Briere, Elizabeth; 91
Byzantine Rite; 2, 89-93, 107, 112,
  116, 117, 131, 157n2


Calvary; 58, 60, 67, 162
Canterbury Cathedral; 136
Capelle, Dom Bernard; 116
*Carême*; 18
Casel, Dom Odo; 82, 163
catechumens; 8, 11, 14, 55, 148, 165
Caxton, William; 68

*Celebrating Easter*; 113, 114, 126, 132, 134, 166
Celebration of the Lord's Passion; 115
Chavasse, Antoine; 77
chrism; 55, 57, 90, 101, 103
Chrism Mass; 99, 101–103, 106
*Christian Year, The* (Keble); 154
Christmas; 76, 129, 159
Cistercians; 160
Commemoration of the Lord's Entry into Jerusalem; 96
Commination Service; 10, 13
Common Prayer, Book of; 7, 10, 21, 54, 78n6, 96, 125, 151, 156
Confession, sacramental; 100
Confirmation; 56, 57, 60, 135, 146n92
Congregation for Divine Worship; 113, 166
Constantine, Emperor; 4, 87, 88
Constantinople; S Saviour-in-Chora; 125
*Constitution on the Sacred Liturgy*; 4, 12, 62, 66n24
Coronation Rite; 122
Covenant; 24, 25, 26, 41
Cranmer, Thomas; 71, 152
Crichton, J. D. 92
Cross; 6, 49, 67-70, 69, 86, 88, 90, 115
  relic of the True; 69, 86, 88, 115
Cross, F. L. 7
*Crux fidelis*; 122
Cullmann, Oscar; 58
Cyril of Jerusalem, S. 9, 85, 87

Davey, Noel; 162
Davis, Charles; 74, 75
death, Christian; 61-62
Decentius, letter to; 115
Devil, the; 14, 15, 37, 55
*disciplina arcani*; 148
*Divine Office*; 15, 18, 19, 69
Dix, Dom Gregory; 85
*Dominica in albis* (Low Sunday); 148
Donne, John; 67-68
Drama; 95, 128, 140
*Dream of the Rood*; 123
Durrwell, F-X; 42, 44, 49, 161, 162
Duruflé, Maurice; 111

Easter; 2, 3, 8, 18, 32, 63, 75, 159, 164, 165
Easter Anthems; 21

Easter Day; 6, 63, 92, 138–141, 148
Easter Eve; 124–126
Easter Garden; 128
Easter Octave; 148
Easter Sepulchre; 128
Easter Vigil; 6, 7, 9, 19, 22, 45, 46, 47, 76, 80, 82, 85, 91, 101, 104, 106, 115, 116, 118, 119, 126–138, 139, 166. (see also Paschal Vigil)
Eastertide; 148-157
Ecumenical Movement; 163
Egeria; 9, 85, 87, 88, 112, 115, 117, 139, 142n15, 148
*electi*; 8, 133
Elijah; 30, 39
Eliot, T. S. 76
*Eostre*; 18
*epitaphion*; 90, 91
Eucharist; 40, 42-43, 59, 60, 61, 64, 70, 100, 101, 105, 108, 110, 126, 148
Evening Prayer, (Anglican); 19, 124, 140, 141
Exaltation of the Holy Cross; 90
Exodus, Book of; 18, 19, 20, 29, 91, 108, 119, 126
event; 18, 19, 23-25, 27, 28, 29, 35, 41, 44, 45, 46, 67
*Exsultet*; 19, 28, 45, 46, 122, 127, 128, 131, 132

fasting; 2, 9, 11, 12, 15, 115, 116, 148, 151
*Festum Festorum*; 5
'Fig' Monday; 98
font; 54, 55, 57, 62, 65n6, 134, 135, 141
footwashing; see Washing of the Feet.
Franciscans; 160
Friedlander, Albert; 30
funerals; 62

Gelasian Sacramentary; 93, 99, 101, 117
General Synod of the C of E; 2, 122
Gennep, Arnold van; 164
Gerhard, Paul; 119
Gethsemane; 86, 112
*Gloria in excelsis Deo*; 133
'glorious office'; 141
*Golden Legend*; 68
Golgotha, (*gulgulta*); 68, 84, 86, 88, 115

Good Friday; 6, 48, 69, 74, 76, 86, 90, 114-124, 127, 166
'Good Shepherd' Sunday; 150
Gospel of the Watch; 114
Great Fifty Days; 6, 148-158
Grünewald, Matthias; 160

*Haggadah*; 28, 29, 30
Harrowing of Hell; 125
*Heilsgeschichte*; 28
Helena, S. 87, 88
Herbert, George; 10, 125
Hippolytus; 7, 8, 130
Holy Places; 87, 149
Holy Saturday; 124-126
Holy Week; 2, 6, 18, 22, 35, 48, 64, 75, 76, 77, 80-141, 149, 150, 163, 164, 166, 167
Hooke, S. H. 39
Hoskyns, Sir Edwin; 162

iconography, of the Passion; 59, 69, 119-120, 159, 160, 162
of the Resurrection; 91, 125
*Improperia*; see *Reproaches*
Initiation, Christian;7, 8, 56, 130, 133, 134, 135-136
Innocent I, Pope; 115
Innocent III, Pope; 116
Intercessions; 132 (See also Solemn Prayers)
Irenaeus, S. 6, 78n2, 154
Istanbul—Karije Museum; 125

Jeremias, Joachim; 39, 137
Jerome, S. 131, 137
*Commentary on S. Matthew*; 137
Jerusalem; 35, 36, 54, 82, 83, 85, 87, 88, 93, 95, 96, 112, 115, 117, 118, 121, 130, 139, 148
Jesuits; 114
John the Baptist; 37, 44, 48, 55
John Chrysostom; 58, 92
*Homilies on S. John's Gospel* 58
liturgy of; 92
John Paul II; 134, 136
Jonah, Song of; 37, 38
Jones, David; 164
Josephus; 29
Judas; 107, 122
Jung, Carl G. 165
Jungmann, Josef, SJ. 85, 116
Justin Martyr; 47

Keble, John; 154

Kempis, Thomas à 160
'Kenotic Hymn'; 97, 109
*koinonia*; 110

*laetissimum spatium*; 148, 149
Last Supper; 26, 39-42, 107, 108
Lateran Basilica; 141
Lent; 1-16, 18, 67
*LHWE*; 12, 13, 30, 62, 80, 81, 94, 95, 96, 97, 99, 103, 108, 111, 112, 114, 116, 118, 122, 127, 129, 130, 132, 136, 140, 141, 150, 151, 152
Leo, Pope S. 76, 89, 93, 98, 134
Lewis, C. S. 111
Lima Report; see *Baptism, Eucharist, Ministry*
Litany of the Saints; 135
liturgical colours; 62, 94, 97, 151
Liturgical Movement; 81, 163
liturgical reform; 4, 80-82, 103, 150
liturgical year; 3, 77
Lord's Supper, Mass of the; 99, 105, 107, 108
Low Sunday; 150
*Lucernarium*; 130, 131
Lugano Congress; 116

*Magna Dominica*; 148
Maimonides, Moses; 154
*Maison-Dieu, la*; 82
Manichees; 14
*mandatum novum*; 109, 110
Maria-Laach; 82, 163
Martin, J. T. 112
Maundy Thursday; 19, 86, 99, 104, 105-114
McArthur, A. A.; 5, 8
Melito of Sardis; 20, 22, 26, 138
memorial—see *anamnesis*
Milner-White, Eric; 99
*Missa Chrismatis*; 99, 101
Missal, the Roman; 9, 21, 78n2, 80, 99, 106, 153, 156
Moléon, Sieur de; 141
Montefiore, Bishop Hugh; 122
Morning Prayer (ASB); 18, 124
Mount of Olives; 83, 86
mystery; 70-74

narrative theology; 25, 33n9, 33n12
Neale, J. M. 21
New Fire; 127, 131
Nicaea—First Council of; 1, 3, 6, 82
Second Council of; 121

20th Canon of; 148, 149
Nicholson, Norman; 54
Nocent, Adrian; 75, 98

O'Collins, Gerald; 167
Octave of Easter; 148
Octave of Pentecost; 151
Office Hymns; 21, 48
Office of Readings; 15, 18, 48, 69, 125, 154
*O filii et filiae*; 141
Oils, the Holy; 102–103
*Order for the beginning of Lent, LHWE*; 12
*Ordo Paenitentiae (1973)*; 13, 100. see also Penitential Services
*Ordo Romanus XXVII*; 141
*O Rex Gloriae*; 152
Origen; 22, 23
Orthodox Church; 1, 9, 31, 89–92, 136, 139, 163

palm cross; 94
Palm Gospel; 96
Palm Sunday; 85, 93–98, 99, 128
*Pange lingua gloriosi Corporis*; 113
*Pange lingua gloriosi proelium*; 48, 69, 122, 124
*Pâques*; 18
*paradosis*; 107
Paris; 141
*Parousia*; 63, 72, 96, 132
*Pascha*; 4, 5, 6, 8, 9, 16, 18, 22, 76, 77, 148, 149, 153, 155, 157
Paschal Candle; 45–47, 62, 75, 127, 128, 131–132, 133, 135, 136, 138, 141, 150
Paschal Eucharist; 137, 138
Paschal Gospel; 44
Paschal Lamb; 5, 21, 23, 25, 29, 41, 43, 45, 47
Paschal Mystery; 3, 13, 16n7, 18, 61, 64, 70, 72, 74, 76, 93, 95, 98, 136, 139, 149, 155, 168
Paschal Proclamation; see *Exsultet*
Paschal Vigil; 6, 7, 8, 14, 18, 77, 93. See also Easter Vigil
Passion of Christ; 59, 98, 159, 160
—Good Friday; 119
—Palm Sunday; 97–98
Passion Sunday; 93
Passiontide; 67,78n1, 93
Passover, Christian; 4, 5, 18, 19, 23, 28, 52–64

Passover. of Christ; 22. 35-50. 52, 64
Passover, Jewish; 18–3?, 35, 64, 126, 137, 148, 154
Passover Lamb: see Paschal Lamb
Passover meal; 19. 28. 29
Paul VI, Pope; 9, 77, 80, 102, 105
Penance, private; 13, 99-101
   public; 10–11
Penitential Services; 13
Pentecost; 6, 57, 128, 149, 150, 151, 152, 153, 154, 157
*Peregrinatio Aetheriae*; 85. see also Egeria
Peter Chrysologus; 15
Pézeril, Daniel; 129
Philo; 29
*Phos hilaron*; 131
Pius V, Pope; 132
Pius XI, Pope; 122
Pius XII, Pope; 80, 91, 97, 132, 141
Poitiers; 69
Polycarp, S. 5
Polycrates, Bishop of Ephesus; 6
*Pontificale Romanum*; 10, 100
Presanctified, Mass or Liturgy of the; 81, 90, 114, 116
Prideaux, Dom Denys; 73
priesthood; 102, 103, 106.
procession, Palm Sunday; 94, 97

*Quadragesima*; 18
Quartodecimans; 5, 6, 16n12, 22
*Quem quaeritis*; 140
Qumran; 72

Ramsey, A. M. 43, 64, 73, 74, 119, 162
Ravenna; 15, 69
Reconciliation of Penitents; 10, 13, 99, 100
Red Sea; 19, 21, 22, 24, 25, 29, 37, 46, 54, 91
Reformation; 6, 12, 165
*Regina Coeli*; 91
Reichenau, Abbey of; 111
Renewal of Baptismal Promises; 9, 14, 134, 135, 136, 140, 141
Renewal of Priestly Commitment; 102
*Reproaches, the*; 90, 121, 122
Reserved Sacrament; 106, 115, 116, 117

*Rite of Christian Initiation of Adults (RCIA)*; 8, 17n14, 146n92, 165
rites of passage; 164–165
Rome; 10, 88, 119, 139, 140
Rogation Days; 151
rosary; 70
Rouen Cathedral; 141
Royal Maundy; 143n42
Russian Orthodox Church; 1, 31, 91

Sacraments; 58, 64, 148
*Sacrosanctum Concilium*; see Constitution on the Sacred Liturgy;
Saints, commemoration; 4, 82
*Santa Croce in Gerusalemme*; 88
Schmemann, Alexander; 1,14
*Seder*; 28, 31
*Sequence*; 48, 139, 140
Service of Light; 127, 129, 130–132, 156
Sessorian Palace; 88
*Shepherd of Hermas*; 15
'Shere' Thursday; 99
Sinai, Mount; 24, 41, 154, 155
Solemn Prayers; 115, 120
sprinkling; 59, 136, 140
'Spy' Wednesday; 98
Stanbrook Abbey; 32
Stational Masses; 98, 99
Stations of the Cross; 114, 159
Stendahl, Krister; 119
Stripping of the altars; 113
symbolism; 128–129, 164
*synaxis*; 115, 118
Syria, Church in; 85, 137
Sylvester I, Pope S. 88

Tabernacles, feast of; 152
Taizé; 51n17, 134, 142n14, 163
Talley, Thomas J. 5, 16n12, 40, 85, 142n10, 152.
Temple, Jerusalem; 36, 59
Tertullian; 7, 22, 58, 148
   *De Baptismo*; 7, 157n1
   *De Anima*; 58
*tesserakoste*; 2

Three Hours' Devotion; 114
Tillich, Paul; 165
*traditio*; 107
Transfiguration of Christ; 38–39
*transitus*; 22, 29, 35, 43, 47, 53, 61, 74, 77, 88, 93, 128, 165
Tree of life; 68
*triduum*; 93, 99, 103–105, 124, 139, 140, 164, 167
Trinity, the Holy; 52, 74
Trinity Sunday; 151
*Trisagion*; 91, 121
trope; 140
typology; 22, 23, 54

*Ubi caritas*; 111
Urban II, Pope; 11

Vatican II (Second Vatican Council); 4, 11, 12, 77, 80, 105, 150
veiling of images; 75, 78n1, 93
Venantius Fortunatus; 48, 69, 122
Veneration of the Cross; 48, 74, 81, 86, 88, 90, 115, 116, 120–123
Venice; 125
Vespers; 48, 90, 91, 140, 141
*Vexilla Regis*; 48, 119
*Victimae Paschali*; 48, 140
Victor I, Pope; 5
*Vidi aquam*; 59, 136, 140
Vigil of Pentecost; 156
Voragine, Jacobus de; 68

Ware, Bishop Kallistos; 90
Washing of the Feet; 90, 108–112, 143n41
Watch, Maundy Thursday; 112–114
   —Gospel of; 114
water; 37, 54-59, 134-136
Watts, Isaac; 159
Weeks, feast of; 152, 153
Westcott, B. F. 162
Weston, Frank; 112
Whit-Sunday; 156
Williams, Charles; 14
Wipo; 48, 140
wisdom; 71–72

# Index of Scriptural References

**OLD TESTAMENT**

**Genesis**
| | |
|---|---|
| 1 | 132 |
| 9:9–17 | 25 |
| 15:18 | 25 |

**Exodus**
| | |
|---|---|
| 3:10 | 23 |
| 5:2 | 23 |
| 7–10 | 23 |
| 12 | 18 |
| 12:5 | 23 |
| 12:11 | 29 |
| 12:33 | 24 |
| 12:42 | 126 |
| 12:46 | 43 |
| 13:21 | 24 |
| 14 | 18, 132 |
| 14:5–31 | 24 |
| 15:22–25 | 67 |
| 19:5–6 | 24 |
| 24:3–8 | 41 |
| 24:7–8 | 24 |

**Numbers**
| | |
|---|---|
| 9:12 | 43 |
| 21 | 3 |

**Deuteronomy**
| | |
|---|---|
| 34 | 25 |

**Joshua**
| | |
|---|---|
| 1 | 25 |

**II Kings**
| | |
|---|---|
| 5:1–15 | 3 |

**Job**
| | |
|---|---|
| 7:12 | 37 |

**Psalms**
| | |
|---|---|
| 24:7 | 96 |
| 31 | 118 |
| 42:9 | 37 |
| 69:1 | 37 |
| 118 | 134 |
| 124:3 | 37 |

**Isaiah**
| | |
|---|---|
| 27:1 | 37 |
| 44:3 | 59 |
| 48:20–21 | 29 |
| 50:4–7 | 97 |
| 51:9 | 37 |
| 52:13–53:12 | 118 |
| 58 | 15 |
| 62:11 | 96 |

**Jeremiah**
| | |
|---|---|
| 23:7–8 | 29 |

**Ezekiel**
| | |
|---|---|
| 47 | 3 |
| 47:1–2, 9 | 59 |

**Daniel**
| | |
|---|---|
| 2:18–19 | 72 |
| 9:4–10 | 3 |

OLD TESTAMENT—*cont.*

| Jonah | | | Zechariah | | |
|---|---|---|---|---|---|
| | 2:3-7 | 38 | | 9:9 | 96 |
| | 3:1-10 | 3 | | 12:10 | 121 |
| Micah | | | Malachi | | |
| | 6:3-4 | 121 | | 3:1 | 96 |

NEW TESTAMENT

| Matthew | | | | | |
|---|---|---|---|---|---|
| | 5:20-26 | 3 | John | | |
| | 12:39 | 38 | | 1:9 | 46 |
| | 12:40 | 38 | | 1:14 | 44, 46 |
| | 20:18-19 | 36, 104 | | 1:17 | 47 |
| | 21:1-11 | 96 | | 1:19 | 44 |
| | 21:18-22 | 98 | | 1:29 | 48 |
| | 25 | 137 | | 2:13 | 44 |
| | 25:31-46 | 3 | | 2:19-22 | 59 |
| | 25:35 | 111 | | 2:23 | 44 |
| | 26:14-16 | 98 | | 3:14 | 44 |
| | 26:29 | 42 | | 4 | 3 |
| | 26:30-end. | 114 | | 4:13-14 | 47 |
| | 28:19 | 135 | | 4:22 | 32 |
| | | | | 6:4 | 44 |
| Mark | | | | 6:28-58 | 47 |
| | 1:9-11 | 56 | | 6:48 | 44 |
| | 10:33 | 36 | | 7:37 | 44 |
| | 10:35-40 | 36 | | 7:37-39 | 47, 157 |
| | 10:45 | 48 | | 8:12 | 44, 46, 47 |
| | 11:1-10 | 96 | | 9 | 3 |
| | 14:24 | 41 | | 10:17 | 43 |
| | 14:25 | 42 | | 10:17-18 | 119 |
| | 14:26-end. | 114 | | 11 | 3 |
| | 14:41 | 112 | | 11:52 | 100 |
| | | | | 11:55 | 44 |
| Luke | | | | 12:1 | 44 |
| | 9:31 | 39 | | 12:1 | 44 |
| | 11:29 | 38 | | 12:12-16 | 96 |
| | 11.30 | 39 | | 13 | 108 |
| | 12:35-37 | 132 | | 13:1 | 22, 43, 44, 110 |
| | 12:49-50 | 36 | | 13:8 | 109 |
| | 12:50 | 54 | | 13:34 | 109 |
| | 13:33 | 36 | | 14:28 | 43 |
| | 15 | 3 | | 16:28 | 43 |
| | 18:31-33 | 36 | | 17:1, 13 | 44 |
| | 19:28-40 | 96 | | 18:6 | 119 |
| | 22:14-18 | 42 | | 18:33-38 | 119 |
| | 22:20 | 26 | | 19:30 | 49, 119 |
| | 22:31-62 | 114 | | 19:34 | 58, 59 |
| | 24:25-27 | 39 | | 19:36 | 43, 44 |
| | 24:28-32 | 42 | | 19:37 | 121 |
| | 24:41-43 | 42 | | 19:40 | 119 |

NEW TESTAMENT: John—*cont.*

| | |
|---|---|
| 20:19-23 | 156 |
| 20:22 | 157 |

Acts

| | |
|---|---|
| 1:3 | 149 |
| 1:4 | 42 |
| 2:1 | 149 |
| 4:11-12 | 98,134 |
| 10:41 | 42 |
| 13:33 | 56 |

Romans

| | |
|---|---|
| 4:24-25 | 63 |
| 5:8 | 123 |
| 6 | 134 |
| 6:3-11 | 7, 53 |
| 8:16-17 | 63 |
| 11:2 | 27 |
| 11:29 | 27 |
| 16:25-26 | 72 |

I Corinthians

| | |
|---|---|
| 1:17-31 | 71 |
| 2:6-10 | 72 |
| 3:11 | 134 |
| 4:1 | 70 |
| 5:6-8 | 45 |
| 5:7 | 5, 63 |
| 6:11 | 54 |
| 10:1-4 | 25 |
| 10:2 | 54 |
| 10:11 | 26 |
| 11:24 | 107 |
| 11:25 | 41 |
| 11:26 | 92 |
| 11:27-29 | 111 |
| 13:12 | 72 |
| 15:20 | 154 |
| 15:21 | 68 |
| 15:45 | 155 |

II Corinthians

| | |
|---|---|
| 3:6 | 155 |
| 3:18 | 63 |
| 4:6 | 132 |
| 5:19 | 123 |
| 11:27 | 126 |

Galatians

| | |
|---|---|
| 3:1 | 121 |
| 4:10 | 5 |
| 6:10 | 111 |

Ephesians

| | |
|---|---|
| 1:9 | 70 |
| 1:9-10 | 73 |
| 2:4-6 | 53 |
| 2:20 | 134 |
| 3:4 | 70 |
| 5:14 | 47, 125 |
| 5:32 | 73 |
| 6:19 | 70 |

Philippians

| | |
|---|---|
| 2:5-11 | 97 |
| 2:6-8 | 109 |
| 3:8-11 | 62 |

Colossians

| | |
|---|---|
| 1:13-14 | 56 |
| 1:25-26 | 72 |
| 1:27 | 73 |
| 2:2 | 70 |
| 2:14-15 | 48 |

Titus

| | |
|---|---|
| 3:5 | 54 |

Hebrews

| | |
|---|---|
| 2:14-15 | 48 |
| 4:8 | 47 |
| 4:14-16 | 118 |
| 4:15 | 48 |
| 5:7-9 | 118 |
| 6:4 | 47 |
| 10:32 | 47 |

I Peter

| | |
|---|---|
| 1:3 | 4 |
| 1:3-5 | 50 |
| 1:18-19 | 45 |
| 2:7-8 | 134 |
| 2:22 | 48 |
| 3:20-21 | 54 |

I John

| | |
|---|---|
| 3:2 | 64 |

Revelation

| | |
|---|---|
| 22:1-2 | 59 |
| 22:2 | 67 |